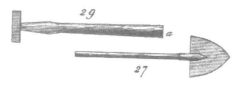

a journey through stone

stone

A JOURNEY THROUGH

Ian Plimer

The Chillagoe Story – the extraordinary history and geology

of one of the richest mineral deposits in the world

REED

Published in 1997 by Reed
a part of Reed Books Australia
35 Cotham Road, Kew, Victoria 3101
a division of Reed International Books Australia Pty Ltd

National Library of Australia
   cataloguing-in-publication data:

Plimer, Ian R.
   A journey through stone: the Chillagoe story: the
   extraordinary history and geology of one of the richest
   mineral deposits in the world.

   Bibliography.
   ISBN 0 7301 0499 0.

   1. Mines and mineral resources – Queensland –
       Chillagoe Region.
   2. Geology – Queensland – Chillagoe Region.
   3. Mineralogy – Queensland – Chillagoe Region.
   4. Chillagoe (Qld.) – History.
   I. Title.

333.85099436

Cover and text designed by Tony Gilevski
Formatting and paging by Mike Kuszla
Printed and bound in Australia by Griffin Paperbacks

CONTENTS

PREFACE

It was a great pleasure to be asked to write the preface to this book. After seeing Ian Plimer's excellent work, *Broken Hill*, I find it most gratifying to think that Chillagoe will also have a chance to show the world its marvellous collection of rare minerals. No one is more qualified to bring this about than Ian, who has worked with Niugini Mining's exploration team in the district since 1991. The mines in the Chillagoe district have uncovered a rich variety of minerals associated with the mining of copper, lead, zinc, gold and silver since their discovery by John Moffat's prospecting teams in 1888.

John Moffat was a visionary developer of North Queensland, having emigrated from Ayrshire, Scotland, in 1862. Having begun his career as a Brisbane storekeeper, tin miner and tin smelter in the Stanthorpe field of southern Queensland, he headed north to Herberton in the Tablelands, behind Cairns, where tin had recently been discovered in 1879. His pioneering capital-raising had reduced working costs to the extent that these remote, non-viable deposits became profitable and supported large communities. He fostered prospecting, smelting and railways, and especially tin mining at Irvinebank, where the Loudon mill and smelting complex treated ores for a century. Named after his mother, the treatment works serviced many of the Atherton Tablelands tin mining centres.

Moffat's 1887 discovery of copper at Chillagoe and Mungana was made viable for mining only by his pioneering endeavours in smelting and railways. I became acquainted with the Herberton tin mines while working there as a geologist in 1977 and it was not until 1990 that I was back in the district again, this time leading a due diligence team to buy out the Red Dome gold and copper mine for Niugini Mining Ltd. One of the great attractions of buying the Red Dome gold mine was that it came with much of the Chillagoe mineral field, and there was clearly great potential to find more mineral deposits.

The skilled workforce and infrastructure were available, and what must have been a daunting, isolated wilderness to the pioneers was now a settled area with modern transport and communications. All that was needed were a vision of the future and the finance to explore and continue to develop the field. This is what Niugini Mining provided – and what it continues to provide, ensuring that the mineral field can be expected to prosper well into the twenty-first century.

This book does a great job of explaining Chillagoe's place in geological history, its rare and beautiful minerals, its colourful past and its future potential. What more could we ask?

GEOFF LOUDON
Former Chairman, Niugini Mining Ltd

ACKNOWLEDGEMENTS

No book can be written without the encouragement, guidance and assistance of others. My initial contact with the Chillagoe field was in the late 1960s when, as a geology research student, I was working in the Featherbed Volcanics and at the Wolfram Camp Mine, north of Dimbulah. Previously, I had been in Broken Hill, the world-famous mining centre in which I was later to work. The fabulous Broken Hill orebody has been the training ground for generations of professionals, many of whom have worked at Chillagoe.

The geological story in this book has been painstakingly compiled by John Nethery. After working for many years on gold prospects in north Queensland and the Mediterranean, and by gaining a scientific understanding of major global geological processes, John has revolutionised the thinking on how the gold ore deposits at Chillagoe formed. All of the geological ideas on the formation of the orebodies at Chillagoe were generated by him and his team. As a result of these new ideas, the life of the mining operations at Chillagoe has been extended, as has employment and the resultant prosperity of the town.

During various trips to Chillagoe, John and Kerry Nethery, the Red Dome Mine, Kerrie, The Black Cockatoo Hotel and the Mount Coonbeter Lodge have looked after me, drunk or sober, and Kerry's brother Alan Bungie Scott proved to be a very patient and skilful helicopter pilot while I was trying to take shots from his Robertson R22. Some of the other geologists in Chillagoe, especially Mike Barr, have shown encouragement and positive criticism of my efforts to communicate the story of Chillagoe.

Both Gavin Thomas, Exploration Director of Niugini Mining Ltd, and Geoff Loudon (former Chairman) have encouraged and assisted this book, as have other Niugini Mining staff such as Mike Christie (Operations Manager) and Ian Goudie (former Chief Executive Officer).

Photographs of some mineral specimens were taken at various museums and thanks are due to Lin Sutherland and Ross Pogson (Australian Museum) and Bill Birch and Frank Coffa (Museum of Victoria). Some of the local collectors, especially Jim Butler, Kevin Crimmin, Kevin Toward and Ned Kelly, gave me permission to photograph their specimens and were very generous with their displays and their time. Pete Williams' interest in the chemistry of natural secondary mineral formation stimulated many changes to the text. All photographs were taken in natural light with a Hasselblad CX500 camera, using Velvia transparencies and an 80-millimetre lens with Proxar lenses and/or bellows. I am grateful to Helen Rowley who drafted all the diagrams.

Acknowledgements

Over the last decade I have been very interested in communicating my science – geology – to lay people who have an interest in nature and in trying to understand how our planet works. I have been greatly encouraged by many people in the media, especially Peter Jeppeson (ABC Regional Radio) and Peter Pockley to get out and sell the fascinating long history of Australia. My summer vacations at Old Bar are therefore spent writing books. This book derives from one such summer of neglecting my family and shunning better offers from my friends, in an attempt to bring the wonders of geology, and minerals, to a wider audience.

INTRODUCTION

Chillagoe is in the headwaters of the Gulf country, about one hundred and fifty kilometres west of Cairns in Queensland. In this book I use the word *Chillagoe* to cover not just the small town of that name but the immediate area around it, for geological processes do not confine themselves to town boundaries. Chillagoe is probably best known for the Chillagoe–Mungana Caves National Park, a spectacular limestone cave system that is a popular destination for tourists.

The story of Chillagoe is written in stone. The rocks provide us with clues to its history, and we must use the methods of a detective to piece them together. Although we were not at the scene of the 'crime', we geologists can assemble these clues to write a history of Australia's exciting past that is beyond reasonable doubt. If more evidence comes to light, then we must refine the picture. But for now we have enough to tell the extraordinary story of Chillagoe, the geological forces that have shaped its minerals, and the wonders that exist there.

What I find remarkable about the Chillagoe area is that it

has been subjected to the same geological processes time and time again, over more than 300 million years. On many separate occasions the rocks have been compressed or stretched; on many separate occasions they have also been broken. And there have been numerous occurrences of volcanic activity. With each separate geological event, a flush of very hot water has passed through the rocks at Chillagoe, causing existing minerals to dissolve and new ones to form. It is these numerous events over a 300-million-year period that have made the place so unique.

The Chillagoe area conjures up many pictures for many people. It is dry, tropical country, known for its cattle and spectacular limestone caves. The area blossoms into life during the wet after the uncomfortable preceding months of hot, humid weather. Green pickings quickly appear, especially in areas burnt in the dry.

The town of Chillagoe has a very rich recent history comprising more than a century of exploration, mining, smelting and associated scandals. Some of Australia's most famous explorers (such as Mulligan), pastoralists (such as Atherton) and prospectors (such as Moffat) are associated with Chillagoe. These pioneers can be credited with the opening up of vast tracts of far north Queensland's very hostile terrain in times when there was no infrastructure. The drive, vision and hardships of such pioneers are too quickly forgotten in the modern world, which has been shaped for us by generations that went before. Some people today regard these pioneers as desecrators of the land; however, the choice in those days was limited – either work or starve.

The mines at Chillagoe are now profitable after more than a century of sporadic activity, financial losses, technical problems and a lack of ore. Numerous eras of mining have been seen here, the best known – the Mungana scandal, in the 1920s – leading to the political downfall of two Queensland premiers.

Chillagoe, in both past and present times, has attracted the best technical brains for mining, smelting and mineral exploration. In the past, these technical people were poached from Broken Hill, causing many promoters to tout Chillagoe as the new Broken Hill. However, while Broken Hill thrived during more than a century of continuous mining, Chillagoe struggled.

Although Chillagoe may have a patchy mining history, it remains a fascinating place for other interest groups.

To mineral collectors, Chillagoe conjures up pictures of world-class crystals of copper minerals, especially cuprite, azurite and malachite. Other collectable minerals are magnificent calcite and garnet crystals and massive copper sulphides. Many rare and interesting minerals are found there.

To many Australians, Chillagoe is best known for its spectacular limestone cave system, with stalactites and stalagmites decorating the huge caverns. These have been hollowed out of the rock by the action of acid water over millions of years, and are a truly awe-inspiring destination to visit.

To geologists, Chillagoe has been perplexing. The early miners found that the erratic nature of the surface outcrops of copper minerals made operations risky. Furthermore, many of the valuable minerals occur at great depths, and the surface offers few clues to their whereabouts. But recently enhanced geological understanding of the Chillagoe area (the result of much research) has enabled a coherent geological history to be constructed, and the pattern of the mineral location to be understood.

The Chillagoe area is one of the most geologically complex areas on planet Earth. Little wonder that more than a century of activity has passed before a plausible geological history can be written. In this book I am attempting to write such a history. I tell the long history of Chillagoe – one where the time span is geological ages – by looking at the stories written for us in stone, and the clues we need to decipher in order to understand why the Chillagoe orebodies are so complex. However, nature is cruel: only some of the clues are there for us to see; others are cleverly concealed.

The long history of the Chillagoe area is not just the result of isolated events in far north Queensland. It is intimately intertwined with the geological history of Australia. The development of many of the features at Chillagoe is directly related to the history of global events such as the drifting of continents.

The latest chapter in the geological history of the area is equally complex and fascinating; it serves to give us an understanding of how the spectacular minerals at Chillagoe formed, and why Chillagoe has caves.

In this book I have also outlined the recent history of Chillagoe, from the first exploration by Europeans to the latest mining ventures – including the successes, the failures and the scandals. No history of Chillagoe would be complete without this outline.

THE LONG HISTORY OF AUSTRALIA

In the beginning . . .

The long history of Australia starts on the moon. The moon shows evidence of an 800-million-year period of intense meteorite bombardment, lasting from about 4500 million years ago until about 3800 million years ago. At this time, the Earth was also being bombarded by meteorites. However, there is a fundamental difference between the Earth and the moon. The moon has never had running water on its surface, whereas the Earth has had running water for at least 3800 million years. Erosion by the water has, over the eons, destroyed the meteorite impact craters on Earth; hence we must go to the moon and the planets of the solar system in order to gain clues about the early history of our solar system.

Soon after the formation of the planets 4500 million years ago, the Earth and the moon both developed iron–nickel cores, and with these a magnetic field. The Earth's magnetic field resulted in a magnetic belt in the upper atmosphere called the van Allen Belt, which filters much dangerous radiation from space, preventing it from reaching the Earth, and so operates as a radiation shield.

In contrast, the moon's core then solidified and it lost its magnetic field. How do we know therefore that the moon ever had a magnetic field? The evidence for this is that lunar rocks contain magnetic minerals which are aligned, indicating that they solidified from a lava – molten rock – which was affected by a magnetic field. We see alignment of magnetic minerals in the Earth's solidified lavas over the history of time. Earth's magnetic mineral alignments show an interesting twist: they have not always been aligned in the present, and expected, north–south orientation. Over the ages, our planet's magnetic field has frequently changed, even sometimes reversing, and the poles have constantly 'wandered around' the Arctic and Antarctic circles.

At one time in Earth's history, when both the temperature of the atmosphere and the planet's surface were less than 100 degrees Celsius, it rained. It rained for the first time. The runoff water removed surface material and deposited it as gravel, sand and silt in river systems and bays. These 3800-million-year-old gravels, which are still preserved in Greenland, not only tell us about the changing atmosphere and surface conditions on Earth, but they also contain evidence of life – the life that first appeared on Earth the minute it rained. The reason Earth sustains life is that, for the last 3800 million years, there has been running water and the van Allen Belt has provided the atmosphere with a protective shield. No other planet in our solar system has such a history. Although it is believed that Mars once had a brief period of running water, some 3600 million years ago, the Earth has had running water for eight-tenths of its history.

The first life on Earth appeared 3800 million years ago and was well established by 3500 million years ago. The earliest life forms on both Earth and Mars were thermophilic (heat-loving) bacteria. Such bacteria, which still exist on Earth today, require no oxygen, and derive heat from hot springs and chemical reactions. Fossil thermophilic bacteria have been found throughout the full 3800-million-year history of life on Earth; excitingly, fossil thermophilic bacteria have recently also been recorded from carbonate inclusions, dated to 3600 million years ago, within a Martian meteorite found in Antarctica.

Thermophilic bacteria are present in the metal-rich, high-temperature, submarine hot springs which occur in the middle of the rifts of mid-ocean ridges, at a water depth of about three kilometres. Modern terrestrial hot springs such as those at Rotorua in New Zealand also contain thermophilic bacteria, which live in very hot, acid, nutrient-rich water there. Deep drilling has shown that thermophilic bacteria also exist many kilometres beneath the surface of the ground, in fractures in the rocks, where they survive on the energy and nutrients released by chemical reactions in the minerals.

Thermophilic bacteria require no oxygen and are therefore classified as anaerobic bacteria. While some people consider humans to be superior organisms, a highly evolved species, I would regard the anaerobic bacteria as the great survivors on planet Earth; they have been in existence for 3800 million years, are still in existence, spanning a great diversity of hostile ecologies. They are the evolutionary success story.

Anaerobic bacteria had the planet to themselves for 1600 million years. During that time they quietly excreted oxygen into the primitive atmosphere as a waste product. At the end of that period, though, there was a profound change in the make-up of the oceans and atmosphere of our planet, resulting in diversification of life. The evidence for this we see in Western Australia.

Oxygen

Three and a half billion years ago, volcanic rocks, sandy and silty sediments and chemical precipitates were laid down in

Western Australia. Only the Pilbara and Yilgarn areas of Australia existed at that time, for the continent had not yet grown to its current size. Colonies of stromatolites (cyanobacteria) thrived in warm, shallow tidal seas; their fossils are now found at Marble Bar in the Pilbara Block and near Kalgoorlie in the Yilgarn Block. Stromatolites still occur in coastal areas of Western Australia.

At that time when anaerobic bacteria were excreting oxygen into the atmosphere, it contained less than 0.1 per cent oxygen, in contrast with the 20 per cent of the modern atmosphere. Ultraviolet light from the sun bombarded sea water and changed some of it to hydrogen and oxygen. The small, light atoms of hydrogen escaped into space, while the heavier oxygen atoms accumulated in the atmosphere. Some of the oxygen atoms combined to form ozone, which greatly reduced the amount of ultraviolet light reaching Earth.

The atmosphere 3500 million years ago contained nitrogen, ammonia, methane, carbon dioxide and the new traces of oxygen, but the anaerobic cyanobacteria did not use oxygen. Once the oxygen in the atmosphere reached a critical concentration, about 2200 million years ago, the Earth experienced an irreversible change: the dissolved iron in the seas rusted as a result of reacting with the oxygen, and in many places the sea floor became covered with an iron oxide–silica sediment. (The banded iron formations of sediment turned into rock which now occupy a large part of the Hamersley Ranges in Western Australia.) At the same time, life expanded to fill the new oxygen-rich ecological niche and aerobic bacteria thrived along with the anaerobic. This was a worldwide event, with the result

6

that aerobic life covered the globe while anaerobic life retreated to more restricted, oxygen-poor environments.

Australia at that time comprised a large part of Western Australia plus small parts of the Northern Territory and South Australia. The anaerobic and aerobic bacteria were the only life on Earth; there were no plants or animals in the oceans or on the land. The continent of Australia was bare. In fact, for eighty per cent of our planet's history, plants did not exist on the continents.

Rifting

The sudden change in the composition of the atmosphere and oceans, and the appearance of aerobic life, was followed by the pulling apart and stitching back together of continents. Some 1800 million years ago the eastern edge of the Australian continent was stretched and a huge rift zone formed. Sediments poured into the rift valley, volcanoes were active and bacterial life thrived on mud flats. The new volcanic rocks were cooled by circulating water, which leached metals from the volcanics and sediments and, in places, redeposited these metals on the rift floor.

A zone of rifting extended from the northern part of the Northern Territory to South Australia, and rocks in the Eyre Peninsula, Yorke Peninsula, Peak and Denison Ranges, Babbage Mountains, Mount Painter at Arkaroola, and in the Olary district, are typical rift sequences. In western New South Wales, the Broken Hill area was once a very deep part of the rift. The rocks at Kakadu, McArthur River and the Jervois Range in the Northern Territory formed in this way 1800 million years ago.

The rocks of the Dargalong Metamorphics, ten kilometres to the west of Chillagoe, also formed in a rift. What were once volcanic and sedimentary rocks were heated at very high pressures, stretched, twisted and bent, and changed to metamorphic rocks. The Mount Isa and Cloncurry areas of northwestern Queensland were formed in the same way, as were the rocks at Georgetown, Einasleigh and Coen in far north Queensland.

In this 1800-million-year-old intracontinental rift, volcanic rocks formed. This happened because, when rifting stretches the Earth's crust, the crust becomes very thin. A decrease in pressure of the underlying hot, high-pressure mantle induces melting, and molten basalt rises along fractures that developed in the rift as the crust was stretched. With the initial stretching of the crust, enormous quantities of molten basalt would have entered the rift as small intrusions and as volcanoes at the edge of the rift. With more intense rifting, even larger masses of very hot molten basalt melted the thin hot lower crust and this molten, crustal material erupted from explosive volcanoes. The more mature rifts were cooled by circulating water which became hot, acid and metal-bearing. When this hot water was expelled as submarine hot springs on the rift floor, metal ores were precipitated. This process occurred at Broken Hill, New South Wales, and in the Cloncurry and Einasleigh districts of Queensland.

The Dargalong Metamorphics

The deep rift that formed in eastern Australia 1800 million years ago was filled with sandy and silty sediment and minor volcanic ash and basalt. The sands and silts were derived from the weathering and erosion of the high volcanic mountains around the rift, which caused massive quantities of sediment to cascade into the rift. (Similar erosion and sedimentation processes are occurring today in the Rift Valley of East Africa, the Red Sea and Lake Baikal in Russia.)

The very thin crust in the rift allowed heat to flow from deep in the Earth, inducing volcanism. Ash and lava erupted from the volcanoes, sediment rapidly filled the deepest part of the rift, and limey, clay-rich muds formed on the tidal flats at its edges. As the rift filled with sediments, it subsided to a great depth, and eventually the sediments and volcanic material in the rift were compressed and heated by the resulting pressure.

The first event of compression and heating took place 1570 million years ago. The rift material was heated to temperatures around 600 degrees Celsius and compressed to four thousand times atmospheric pressure. New minerals, such as garnet, formed in response to the high temperatures and pressure. The rocks lost pore water, and the mineral grains fused onto each other and became elongate. The pressure bent the rocks double, into large folds, and new minerals then grew parallel to the fold axis. The folding pushed up rocks to form a mountain chain – the Dargalong Metamorphics, a very large formation like the Himalayas – to the west of Chillagoe. Before the rocks had a chance to cool down, they were again compressed.

The direction of compression changed and the hot, bent rocks were again bent. The second event of compression took place 1470 million years ago; again the rocks were pushed up into mountains. The rocks were bent double a second time. Then the whole sequence of rocks started slowly to cool. Erosion attacked the tops of the mountains and, as they were ground down, the mountain chain floated up on the mantle, exposing more high-temperature, high-pressure rocks to the forces of erosion.

This process of mountains being pushed up and eroded is taking place throughout the Earth today. India is drifting northwards and colliding with Asia. As a result, the Himalayas are being pushed up: Mount Everest is rising two centimetres per year. At the same time the Himalayas are being ground down by very vigorous erosion due to the fierce weather conditions.

The third deformation of the Dargalong Metamorphics, 970 million years ago, was not as intense as the first two, and the rocks were bent into a corrugated shape. After the third compression there was a 500-million-year period about which we know very little. During this time, either the Dargalong Metamorphics were a stable part of the continent which underwent erosion, or new sediments were deposited on the metamorphics which were removed by later erosion. This sort of patchiness of geological evidence characterises many of our attempts to reconstruct the ancient history of our planet. There are periods of time during which no clues are preserved for one area while we have a continuous record of events for other areas.

We do know that, during the period in which the Dargalong Metamorphics were being formed and shaped, central Australia was stretched, and the continent was in the grip of glaciation.

Elsewhere in Australia – such as western Queensland, the Northern Territory, South Australia and Western Australia – thick sequences of sediments were deposited. In South Australia, a rift started to open 950 million years ago. This was accompanied by thinning of the crust, and basalt volcanoes. Sand, silt and mud poured into the rift, which sank as it was loaded up with sediment.

Icehouse Earth

Around 750 million years ago Earth entered an 'icehouse'. We don't know why, but about every 400 million years for the last 1000 million years there have been regular greenhouses (periods of relatively tropical, wet conditions which occur each time the continents drift apart) and icehouses (periods of relatively cold and dry conditions which occur each time the continents stitch back together). For the bulk of geological time, Earth has had a climate that was warmer and wetter than at present.

Despite the fact that, 750 million years ago, the Australian continent was somewhere near the northern tropics, it too was gripped by the ice. The evidence for an icehouse in the Flinders Ranges of South Australia, then, is unmistakable. Large masses of debris were left behind by retreating glaciers; melt waters washed sand out of this debris, yielding white outwash sands; lakes of melt water formed as a result of the damming of valleys by glacial debris, and these lake sediments contained thousands of layers of winter mud and summer sand. The ancient land surface shows where glaciers polished the rockfaces. The glaciers carried rock debris – fragments and boulders from the land – which scratched the rockfaces. The glaciers dropped into the oceans huge icebergs, also including the debris, and the bergs carried the boulders far out to sea. When the icebergs melted, they dropped the boulders into the muds on the sea floor. Today we can follow the evidence of the glaciers' past by examining the remains of the boulders, and matching them to the area they might have come from.

The explosion of life

When the icehouse ended, about 600 million years ago, both the temperature and the oxygen content of the atmosphere rose. In response, the somewhat simple bacterial life also changed, finding it more efficient to live and die in this new environment as a co-operative group of cells rather than a single-celled organism.

Meanwhile, in the Flinders Ranges 650 million years ago, the first of many great biological experiments had taken place.

This experiment was possible because the oxygen in the atmosphere had risen to almost 1 per cent (in contrast to the present oxygen content of 20 per cent). At 1 per cent oxygen, animals were able to construct the fibrous protein 'collagen', and by doing so they no longer had completely soft bodies. With some structure, such as a skeleton, they could grow bigger and more complex.

The first flourish of life, called Ediacaran fauna, brought forth bizarre biological forms. Large, flat bodies enabled maximum filtration of sea water; as the cells gained nutrients directly from the sea, the organisms had no need for a circulation system and so these animals had no muscles. Some grew gas bladders to enable them to float in the richer, warmer surface waters. Most of these animals became extinct as evolution favoured better methods of feeding and survival, but the modern blue-bottles are a relic of these times.

By 570 million years ago, animal life had developed muscles; the specialised protein ATP, which allows the storage and sudden release of energy; a circulation system; and a diversity of floating, swimming, burrowing, locomotion and feeding techniques. These far more efficient life systems were a revolution in the history of life on Earth. This was the Cambrian explosion of life, an explosion that produced numerous groups of organisms, some of which still exist in evolved forms. But they were all ocean life forms: despite greenhouse conditions, there were still no plants or animals on the continents, and the Australian landscape consisted only of bare rocks and soil.

More than 100 major groups of animals (phyla) appeared in the Cambrian explosion of life 570 million years ago. Since then there have been five major mass extinctions of life on Earth and there is some debate about whether we are in the sixth period. The first mass extinction of life occurred 430 million years ago. Two-thirds of the phyla that had evolved during the Cambrian were wiped out in this event. Ecological niches were vacated, allowing the rapid evolution of new life and its colonisation. Earth continued with its normal business of biological experimentation, extinction and evolution.

The process of evolution over the history of time involves

mutation, natural selection, genetic drift and migration. However, there is another factor – survival of the luckiest. If an organism is lucky enough to survive a mass extinction, then a large number of ecological niches exist for repopulation. There is opportunity for evolution into other forms which capitalise on the vacated niches. We humans evolved from lucky mammals that survived a mass extinction 65 million years ago in which the dinosaurs became extinct.

The average length of life on Earth for a terrestrial species is four million years and, over the 3800-million-year history of life on Earth, one species has become extinct every fortnight. Since the Cambrian explosion of life, some *90 billion* species of life have appeared on Earth. Of these more than 99.9 per cent are now extinct. The bottom line is this: extinction is normal, survival of the species is not.

Part One

THE ANCIENT HISTORY OF CHILLAGOE

The Palmerville Fault

While other parts of Australia were recovering from an ice-house and life was rapidly evolving, intense crustal forces were operating at Chillagoe. Stresses deep in the crust were building up, and the Dargalong Metamorphics first started to stretch then eventually broke. The Palmerville Fault – a curved break in the Earth extending from Princess Charlotte Bay, Cape York, to Halifax Bay, north of Townsville – started to move. This giant break in the Earth's crust has moved many times over the last 600 million years in response to stresses in the crust. The Herbert River has used the Palmerville Fault's weakness as its preferred course, as it is clearly easier for water to cut a course along a fracture than through solid rock.

The Palmerville Fault is so extensive that, like many other distinctive geological features, it is clearly visible from space. East of the Palmerville Fault, we now see no remnants of the Dargalong Metamorphics. However, it is possible that they form the basement to a large basin of sediments, extending from Chillagoe to Cooktown, called the Hodgkinson Basin. Alternatively, as a result of continental drift, the eastern Dargalong Metamorphics may be now be a similar set of rocks in South America.

Throughout the history of deep time, the continents have been drifting apart and stitching back together. When continents start to drift, they break into plates. At one edge, the plate is being extended and pulled apart (constructive plate margin) and at the other end, the plates are being compressed (destructive plate margin). Mid-ocean ridges are modern constructive

million years ago
500
480
460
440
420
400
380
360
340
320
300
280
260
240
220
200
180
160
140
120
100
80
60
40
20
present

17

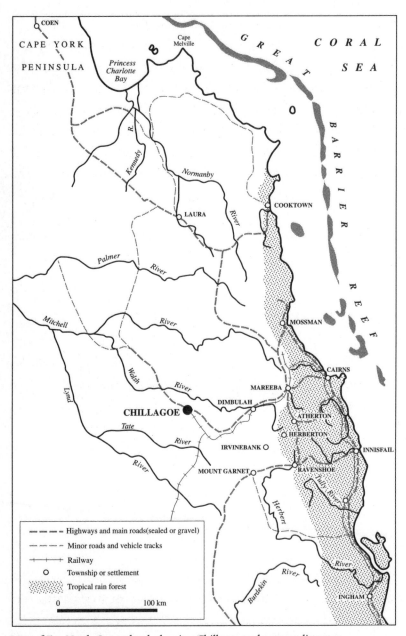

Map of Far North Queensland, showing Chillagoe and surrounding area

plate margins, whereas the arcs of islands in the middle of oceans, and mountain ranges such as the Himalayas and the Andes, are modern destructive plate margins.

Scientists can reconstruct the distribution of land masses for any time during the geological past. They do this by investigating the distribution of rock types, fossils and geological structures, by checking the magnetic orientation of the minerals contained in the rocks (palaeomagnetism) and by dating the rocks by

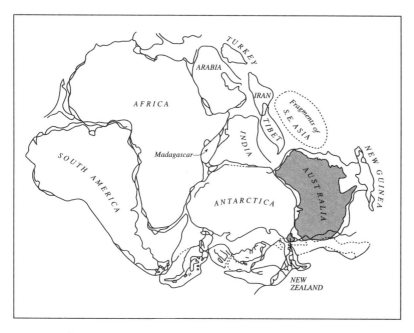

The former giant southern continent, Gondwana

radioactive techniques. Many of the sediments and volcanic rocks (volcanics) at Chillagoe formed while Australia was part of the great southern continent, Gondwana, which at one time included land masses that are now part of Africa, India, Antarctica and South America. The most recent drifting of the continents took place when Gondwana started to break up 180 million years ago; Australia eventually became an island continent 50 million years ago.

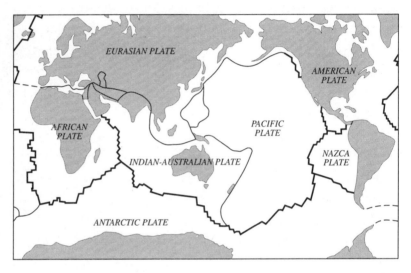

Current configuration of the continents and the current active plate margins

Coastal Chillagoe

If we imagine the Chillagoe area 500 million years ago, west of the Palmerville Fault would have been an elevated or even mountainous area composed of the Dargalong Metamorphics. This elevated area would have had no vegetation, so its erosion would have been accelerated. As soon as there was rain, the erosion would have removed material eastwards from the high-lands into the sea.

To the east of the Palmerville Fault there was a coastal plain, then the continental shelf and ocean deeps called the Hodgkin-son Basin. So Chillagoe would have been on the east coast of Australia with the Palmerville Fault being a prominent coastal scarp. We see such topographic features now in eastern Australia as a result of the relatively recent opening of the Tasman Sea.

Heavy rain and flooding would have brought down masses of gravel and sand from the Palmerville Fault scarp onto the coastal plain (similar pebble and gravel beaches exist in many places where steep mountains abut a stormy coast), and for 150 kilometres on the continental shelf adjacent to the fault scarp, sands, muds and silts were deposited. These sediments either came from a more undulating landscape or had been reworked many times on the beaches at Chillagoe.

The sediment was dumped on to the continental shelf, which became loaded with the unconsolidated muds, silts and sands. During this time, there were active volcanoes and numerous intense earthquakes in the Chillagoe area. Much of the sediment perched on the continental shelf became unstable and it thundered down into the ocean deeps in underwater avalanches. Such submarine avalanches are not uncommon today and, moving at more than 100 kilometres per hour, have been responsible recently for the breaking of trans-oceanic communication cables. The sediments which thundered off the continental shelf at Chillagoe 500 million years ago are now called the Mulgrave Formation.

The presence of basalt and chert in the Mulgrave Formation

500 — million years ago
480
460
440
420
400
380
360
340
320
300
280
260
240
220
200
180
160
140
120
100
80
60
40
20

present

tell another story about coastal Chillagoe 500 million years ago. Basalt is a result of the Earth's crust stretching. When the crust stretches, thins or rifts, the Earth's mantle decompresses and slightly melts. Hot, buoyant, molten rocks ascend fractures and erupt as basalt lava from volcanoes. The presence of basalt in the Mulgrave Formation indicates that the oceans opened up by rifting. The molten basalt was cooled by sea water as it flowed along the sea floor as globules or pillows. Then chemical reactions between the basalt and sea water released silica from the basalt and the silica was deposited on the ocean floor as chert. (We can observe the self-same processes taking place today at mid-ocean ridges.)

Sea level changes

Changes in the sea level 450 million years ago caused reefs, limey muds and sands to form at the edge of the continental shelf. The rocks that are the remains of these materials show that there was a great diversity of shallow-water marine life at that time. Fossils of crinoids, algae, gastropods, ostracods, brachiopods, bryozoans, corals and trilobites have been found in the limestones. Again, we see a similar situation in modern environments: in cold-water habitats only a few species exist, whereas in warm, shallow waters – such as the Great Barrier Reef – there is a great diversity of species. The fossil life in the rocks indicates that the ocean water at Chillagoe 450 million years ago was clear, rich in nutrients and warm.

Ripple marks in sandy rocks and scours on the sea floor show that gentle currents were flowing from the south and south-west. Further out to sea, currents carried sands and gravels off the continental shelf, and fans of sediment formed on the ocean floor from submarine avalanches. For sand and gravel to have been carried by marine currents, the currents would have had to be very strong. These old gravels included boulders that can be traced to the Dargalong Metamorphics, limestones from the reefs at the edge of the continental shelf, granite, and a great variety of volcanic rocks.

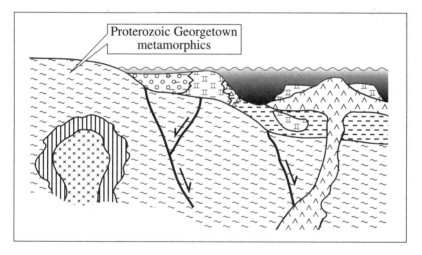

The palaeogeography of the Chillagoe area, 450 million years ago

So we know that Chillagoe 450 million years ago was clearly tropical and coastal. Reconstruction of the continents between 600 and 450 million years ago shows that Australia was in the tropical part of the northern hemisphere. Furthermore, Australia was rotated and slowly drifting northwards.

million
years ago

500
480
460
440
420
400
380
360
340
320
300
280
260
240
220
200
180
160
140
120
100
80
60
40
20

present

23

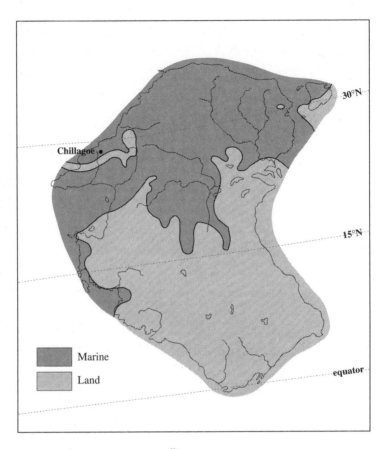

The Australian continent 500 million years ago

Rifting again

Elsewhere in Australia 470 million years ago – in central Australia, the Flinders Ranges and Western Australia, for instance – the rocks were being compressed. This event, known in Australia as the Delamerian Orogeny and internationally as the Pan-African Event, folded rocks twice and heated them until they reached 400 degrees Celsius. In some places in Australia, there was resultant melting of older crustal rocks, which formed granites (for example, Anabama Granite, South Australia) or granites and explosive volcanoes (for example, Arkaroola, South Australia).

The Chillagoe area started to experience yet another event of rifting (not surprisingly, since, as the geological record shows, numerous such events were caused by the constant pulling apart and stitching back together of the Earth's crust). The sea floor was slightly lifted, and to the east of the Chillagoe area the ocean floor was still undergoing rifting. This process resulted in an upward warping of the rift edge (which occurs in rifts today). The Chillagoe Formation was then deposited in the extensive shallow seas on this upwarped rift edge.

How would the Chillagoe Formation have manifested itself? The answer is: as atolls fringing basalt volcanoes, little different from islands in the present-day tropical Pacific Ocean. The basalt volcanic remains at Chillagoe have the chemistry of modern basalt volcanoes which occur at mid-ocean ridges. Furthermore, the chemistry of the basalts shows that they have derived from the slight melting of the Earth's mantle, a result of stretching of the crust during rifting, and that no continental crust had melted or been mixed up with the molten basalt. This again suggests that the basalt volcanoes were islands out in the ocean well away from the continent. So, the 450-million-year-old basalts at Chillagoe are from islands like Lord Howe Island or Tonga, where coral reefs wrap around a basalt volcano.

The stretching of the crust was a result of diagonal tensional forces. Many of the rocks in the old continent to the west,

500 $\frac{\text{million}}{\text{years ago}}$

480

460

440

420

400

380

360

340

320

300

280

260

240

220

200

180

160

140

120

100

80

60

40

20

present

composed of the Dargalong Metamorphics, show fractures trending north-easterly as the tension induced a breakage of rocks which then slid past each other. This tension started in the Chillagoe area 470 million years ago and continued for 100 million years. Many of the ancient volcanoes in the Chillagoe area occurred along these north-easterly fractures. Molten rock has great difficulty rising through solid rock but once there are prominent fractures, these become the channelways for hot, buoyant masses of molten rock.

Tensional forces have occurred throughout the history of time – and still occur in many parts of Australia, producing sporadic earthquakes. Similar tensional force release and the sliding of rocks are currently occurring in many places around the world, such as the San Andreas Fault in California.

Chillagoe limestones

The ancient fringing reefs contained a diversity of life, as evidenced by the fossils. Some of these life forms, such as trilobites and graptolites, are now extinct. Graptolites became extinct in the first of our planet's five mass extinctions, 430 million years ago, whereas trilobites survived on Earth until the third mass extinction, 245 million years ago. Trilobites constitute three-quarters of the fossil species found in the Cambrian period following the explosion of life 570 million years ago, and they became extinct in a crisis of life in which 96 per cent of all Earth species were wiped out. The reason for this mass extinction is not known.

The atolls at Chillagoe were ringed by fragments of broken reef material left by storms that had battered the middle to outer reefs close to the edge of the continental slope. In deep water around the atolls, limey muds with reef debris predominated (the Great Barrier Reef today has similar outer and inner reefs ringed by broken reef debris). This fringing reef and associated limey material have become the limestone of Chillagoe.

The Chillagoe Formation contains other sediments characteristic of deep water conditions. Among these are fine-grained, silty sediments which settled on the ocean floor after the currents had swept muds and clays from shallow water into deep water. There is also well-layered chert, a sedimentary rock composed of silica, which is formed by the sinking and accumulation of silica shells from floating animals called radiolaria.

The ocean deeps

The continental shelf was draped with muds, silts and sands. In an earthquake-prone area, these unconsolidated sediments were unstable. Submarine avalanches of shallow-water sediments and fringing reef material would have redeposited unconsolidated sediments in the ocean deeps. The occurrence of large blocks of shallow water limestone in the deep-water sediments demonstrates the force of the submarine avalanches at that time. These avalanches probably thundered down submarine canyons as they do today.

Modern submarine canyons contain gravels which are moved along the canyon floor by strong currents and, where the canyon

500 million years ago
480
460
440
420
400
380
360
340
320
300
280
260
240
220
200
180
160
140
120
100
80
60
40
20
present

meets the ocean deeps, sediments fan out onto the ocean floor. These sediments contain large fragments close to the canyon mouth and progressively smaller fragments progressively further away from the canyon mouth. This pattern is exactly what has been found in the sediments of the Chillagoe Formation. Because large blocks of Chillagoe limestone are found in these deep-water sediments, we know that the submarine slope from the fringing reefs to the ocean deeps must have been very steep.

But there are also other clues. Fragments of continental material in the rare conglomerates in the Chillagoe Formation, which were formed from gravels in the deep submarine canyons, indicate that, 450 million years ago, the east coast of the continent was deeply incised. Rapid erosion of the continent shed gravel into fast-flowing rivers, which left gravel sheets on the continental shelf. These gravel sheets were shifted down the continental slope into the submarine canyons.

In the ocean deeps, a very large area of grey sands and muds was deposited by the submarine avalanches, which spread sediment over hundreds of kilometres across the ocean floor. Over a long period of time, as the continent to the west was eroded during the warm, wet conditions, this resulted in the accumulation of a thick sequence of rocks formed from the sediments. Rare coarse-grained conglomerates have been found towards the base, along with minor basalt and radiolarian chert. The basalt indicates that the ocean floor was still being stretched by rifting, molten basalt rising up through fractures in the rift and freezing in the wet, ocean-floor sediments. This sequence of rocks, called the Hodgkinson Formation, covers an extensive area to the east of Chillagoe.

Meanwhile, shallow-water tropical sediments and deep-water

ocean-floor sediments filled the rift to the east of the shoreline. West of the shoreline was the continent, composed of the Dargalong Metamorphics. The continent had undergone intense weathering and erosion each time it was uplifted – a slice of the continental crust at least 8 kilometres thick had been planed off the Dargalong Metamorphics during a 100-million-year period of intense weathering and erosion from 550 to 450 million years ago. As there was neither plant nor animal life on the continent 450 million years ago, soil was not stabilised and the erosion of tropical Chillagoe, along with all other landmasses, was far more rapid than it is today.

As a result, the Dargalong Metamorphics, once steep mountains, were planed into gently undulating hills. Because mountains float on more plastic rocks deep below them, when their peaks are eroded, they rise. This allows high-pressure, high-temperature rocks to be exhumed from a great depth to the surface. (It is by this mechanism that we are able to look underneath Himalayan mountains.) As rocks are exhumed, they depressurise and crack. These cracks allow water to percolate through them, which accelerates erosion.

Molten rock at Chillagoe

The tensional stresses in the Dargalong Metamorphics, combined with the north-easterly fractures and the uplift of more than eight kilometres, enabled melting to take place at depth. The molten rocks which formed were light and moved up along fractures in the Dargalong Metamorphics.

million
years ago
500
480
460
440
420
400
380
360
340
320
300
280
260
240
220
200
180
160
140
120
100
80
60
40
20
present

29

Molten granite contains some dissolved water. As molten rock rises, the water separates from the rock as very hot steam and the steam flushes metals out of the molten rock. The molten rock in the Dargalong Metamorphics froze solid, 430 million years ago, some kilometres beneath the surface, to form the Nundah Granodiorite. But when the rock froze, the metal-rich steam moved into the surrounding Dargalong Metamorphics. In the Dargalong Metamorphics are high-temperature, high-pressure minerals which were formed 1570 million years ago during intense compression. This compression drove water out of the Dargalong Metamorphics. The metal-rich steam released from the Nundah Granodiorite 430 million

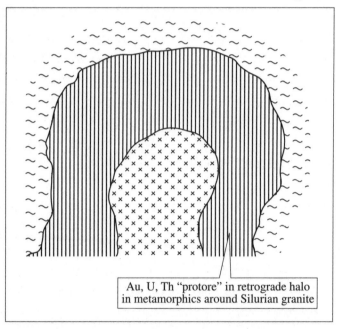

Au, U, Th "protore" in retrograde halo in metamorphics around Silurian granite

The mineral deposits associated with the Nundah Granodiorite in the Chillagoe area, 450 million years ago

years ago formed a halo of water-rich minerals in the Darga-long Metamorphics: a halo glinting with uranium, thorium and gold. In the halo are fractures filled with quartz and traces of gold. Modern weathering has released the gold from some of these veins, and it has been concentrated in streams draining from the halo around the Nundah Granodiorite.

The Nundah Granodiorite is strongly non-magnetic, contain-ing the non-magnetic iron-oxide mineral, ilmenite, so some of the geology of the areas can be determined from aerial surveys. (Because much of Australia is covered with a thick weathered profile or wind-blown sand, aeromagnetics is a standard tech-nique used to see beneath the surface and to map the major geo-logical features.) We discover from the surveys that every twenty kilometres parallel to the Palmerville Fault, on both the east and west side of it, there is strongly non-magnetic rock covered by younger, more magnetic material. These magnetic anomalies may be unexposed masses of Nundah Granodiorite. However, the fact that they are parallel to the Palmerville Fault indicates that the fault exerted significant control on the rising of molten rocks from depth. This is not surprising, as molten rock moves up fractures rather than pushing its way through solid rock.

While the huge mass of molten rock was moving upwards along fractures in the Dargalong Metamorphics at Chillagoe, 430 million years ago, other changes were taking place on the continents, and these were related to changes in the oceans and atmosphere. Early Earth, as I have explained, had very little oxy-gen in its atmosphere, and as soon as there was a minor oxygen content, anaerobic bacteria evolved. Once the oxygen content of the atmosphere reached about 1 per cent, there was an explosion of life. When the oxygen in the atmosphere increased to more than 10 per cent, some 430 million years ago, another profound change took place: the continents started to become colonised with land plants. Some of the oldest land plant fossils have been found in Victoria.

The colonisation was not only due to the increased oxygen content of the atmosphere; it was given a helping hand by a mass extinction of animal life in the oceans at the same time. Without animals eating the plant life, the seas were becoming crowded, and the uninhabited, warm, wet continents were an ideal ecological niche to fill. The colonisation of continents by plants created additional food sources, and animals started to forage on the tidal mudflats above the waterline. So, once the land was colonised by plants, a whole new ecology was opened up for exploitation by animals, which in turn left their marine environments.

The Murchison Gorge, Western Australia, boasts the oldest animal tracks on tidal flats on Earth. These are of giant, scorpion-like marine predators in 400-million-year-old mudstones. The predators had evolved from purely marine environments to a life where they could benefit from both marine and terrestrial ecologies.

The bending of Chillagoe

Between 420 and 380 million years ago, the Australian continent was located in the northern hemisphere. However, continental Australia was now drifting southwards and rotating in a clockwise direction. Eventually, 370 million years ago, Australia could be described as part of an equatorial mass bisected by the equator.

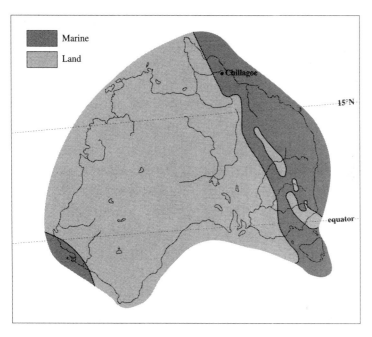

The Australian continent 380 million years ago

After this 100-million-year period of tension, during which the Nundah Granodiorite formed, the tensional forces changed direction. (Moving, twisting, turning and buckling of continents is quite normal and tensional forces often change direction.) This change in direction resulted in compression, which folded and bent double the whole sequence of rocks that had formed in the water off the coast. The sediments and volcanics formed in the rift between 470 and 370 million years ago were now stitched onto the continent of Australia. It has been by this process that the continent of Australia has been able to grow eastwards over the last 500 million years. Currently, around the Pacific Ocean, island arcs such as Japan are growing eastwards and, to the west, stitching onto the Chinese mainland in just the same way.

The compression occurred all along eastern Australia and is called the Kanimblan Orogeny, after an area near Bathurst in New South Wales. The compression 370 to 325 million years ago at Chillagoe was so great that the rocks not only bent, but they broke. The old major weakness in the crust, the Palmerville Fault, was re-broken, reactivated and moved.

The sequence of rocks next to the Palmerville Fault was broken into slices which were pushed up on top of each other (just like what happens when a pack of cards is pushed sideways). Slices of the Dargalong Metamorphics were humped on top of a sequence of packed slices of the Chillagoe Formation. Normally, younger sediments are laid upon older rocks; however,

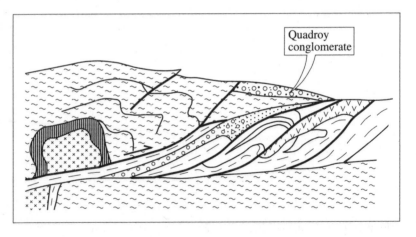

The slicing up of the Chillagoe area between 370 and 325 million years ago

when rock sequences are sliced up, it is not uncommon to have slices of older rocks pushed over younger rock, as has happened in the Alps of Europe.

Then the Nundah Granodiorite broke in half. Some of the uranium, thorium and gold deposited in the halo around it, 450 million years ago, were flushed out, moved along the Palmerville Fault and redeposited in the rocks above the fault.

In both modern and ancient environments, each time crustal material fails after having been stressed for a long period of

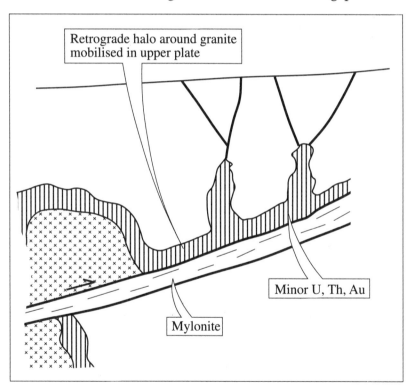

Retrograde halo around granite mobilised in upper plate

Minor U, Th, Au

Mylonite

The redeposition of uranium, thorium and gold during movement along the Palmerville Fault 370 to 325 million years ago

500 million years ago
480
460
440
420
400
380
360
340
320
300
280
260
240
220
200
180
160
140
120
100
80
60
40
20
present

time, the rocks break along faults, and earthquakes occur. Hot water is then pumped along the fault. Each time the rocks in the Chillagoe area broke, the Palmerville Fault moved, branched and had hot waters pumped along it. The hot waters carry metals in solution which have been flushed from one site and may be deposited in a concentrated form elsewhere.

The outcrop pattern of limestones in the Chillagoe area reflects the thrusting of slices of rocks on top of each other. Fossiliferous limestones of the Chillagoe Formation occur as discontinuous ridges, which are really slices of limestones packed upon each other like a pack of cards. Faults separate these ridges, which are stacked parallel to each other. These characteristics are very evident from the top of any hill in the Chillagoe area or from the air. (See colour plate 1)

The compression 370 to 325 million years ago was a major mountain-building process. Similar compression, forming mountains, is currently occurring as a result of the northward flight of India from Australia to collide with Asia: the Himalayas have risen at the collision zone. In the Himalayas, numerous earthquakes occur from the breaking of rocks during collision, and the mountains are currently being pushed up, with Mount Everest rising two centimetres per year. Massive erosion is taking place to form extensive gravels which will eventually be solidified into conglomerate.

The Chillagoe area became mountainous in the same way, the compression pushing rocks up into a mountain chain along the length of eastern Australia. These mountains started to erode rapidly, causing gravel to be draped over the mountain slopes and shed into fast-flowing rivers, and these products of erosion wave eventually deposited in the deltas of major rivers draining from the mountain chain. The gravel sheets were washed off the mountains for some two hundred kilometres along the Palmerville Fault. These gravels have now been hardened and are called the Quadroy Conglomerate.

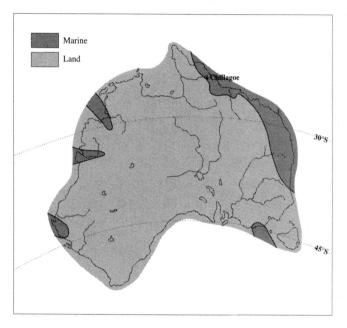

The Australian continent 325 million years ago

While the Kanimblan Orogeny was taking place in eastern Australia, life in Australia was changing. The second of the global major mass extinction events took place 368 million years ago, possibly as a result of a giant meteorite which struck Siljan, Sweden, leaving a 52-kilometre-wide crater. Another impact 360 million years ago left a 46-kilometre-wide crater in Charlevoix, Quebec, Canada. Craters must be at least thirty-two

million
500 years ago
480
460
440
420
400
380
360
340
320
300
280
260
240
220
200
180
160
140
120
100
80
60
40
20
present

kilometres in diameter in order to cause a 'significant biological effect', defined as a mass extinction of ten per cent of life on Earth. Craters of about fifty kilometres in diameter, such as those in Canada and Sweden, lead to a mass extinction of thirty per cent of life on Earth.

The chance combination of these two meteorite impact events in Sweden and Canada, so close together, would have been catastrophic for life on Earth. The impacts would have ejected into the atmosphere huge amounts of dust, which would have prevented most sunlight reaching Earth. Furthermore, the collapse back to Earth of rock fragments and dust from the craters would have significantly raised the atmospheric temperature, due to frictional heat, and much life would have been cooked to extinction. Events of mass extinction are followed by periods of very rapid evolution, and the lucky surviving organisms would have rapidly filled the vacated ecologies.

In inland Australia 360 million years ago, arid conditions prevailed, causing the era to be known geologically as the age of the fishes. However, the inland lakes dried up, resulting in giant fish kills which are in evidence today in numerous fish fossil localities. The best known of these, at Canowindra, New South Wales, contains thousands of fish fossils, including extinct armoured fish and air-breathing lobe-finned fish. It is one of the world's greatest fossil deposits.

In eastern Victoria 360 million years ago, a four-legged animal with five toes on each foot and a tail or dragging belly left its imprints in muds. The muds were later covered by silts and the footprints remained. This amphibian left the oldest four-legged tracks known on Earth and heralded the start of the colonisation of the continents by animals.

After the bending

500 — million years ago
480 —
460 —
440 —
420 —
400 —
380 —
360 —
340 —
320 —
300 —
280 —
260 —
240 —
220 —
200 —
180 —
160 —
140 —
120 —
100 —
80 —
60 —
40 —
20 —
present

When the plates of the Earth move and collide, the direction of stress changes and the plates close like scissors (which happens only if two plate edges are pushed into each other *at an angle*; it does not happen if they are parallel). At one end, compression occurs and at the other, extension. Furthermore, the collision of plates at an angle produces a lull in stress. Such lulls commonly occur as the direction of stress rotates. This is exactly what happened 325 to 315 million years ago, as the rock stresses greatly decreased following the mountain-building associated with the Kanimblan Orogeny.

In this particular lull, the mountains composed of the Dargalong Metamorphics and the sliced-up Chillagoe Formation continued to be cut down by weathering and erosion, and fans of gravel continued to be spread out from the Palmerville Fault. Again, as the mountains were eroded, they buoyantly rose. The Australian landmass continued to drift southwards until it was in a subpolar position. It also continued to rotate clockwise, which resulted in compression, plate collision, folding and volcanicity.

At that time, because slices of the crust had been humped onto each other, the Earth's crust at Chillagoe was very thick. The bottom of the crust was cooked at high pressures. The lull in stress caused large parts of the crust to sink and, as sinking continued, the crust started to stretch. Eventually, after much stretching, the rocks broke into a sequence of sunken and elevated blocks. (This same process occurs in modern rifts.)

Stretching thinned the crust and resulted in the formation of molten rock at depth. Molten rock is less dense than its solid equivalent, and the density of the molten rock is further decreased because gases such as steam and carbon dioxide are dissolved in it. Less dense material rises above dense material, so molten rock tends to rise. The molten rock rose from deep in the crust via fractures and faults, some of it freezing before it reached the surface, to form huge masses of granite, but most of it erupting on the surface via volcanoes.

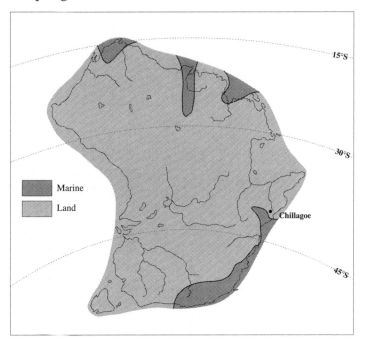

The Australian continent 300 million years ago

As the molten rock was rising, it was also cooling. Crystals of quartz and feldspar started to grow and bob around in the rock. When it finally froze, the resulting solid rock – of the type known as porphyry – thus consisted of coarse-grained crystals in a fine-grained ground mass. Some molten rock froze in the fractures to form wall-like masses, called dykes. The porphyry dykes at Chillagoe – at their best in the Red Dome open pit – are narrow and discontinuous.

Together, these granites, volcanics and porphyries at Chillagoe, which solidified in the stress lull 325 to 315 million years ago, constitute the geological phenomenon known as the O'Briens Creek Supersuite.

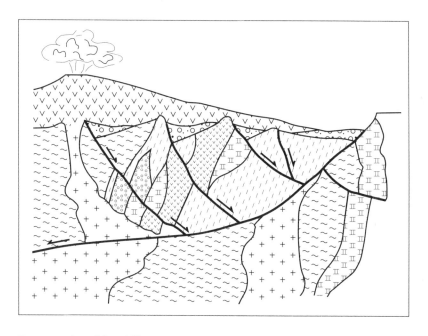

Reconstruction of the Chillagoe area, 325 to 315 million years ago

Steam and ore

The O'Briens Creek Supersuite is unusual in several respects.

Instead of containing the magnetic iron oxide mineral called magnetite, as does the 430-million-year-old Nundah

million
500 years ago
480
460
440
420
400
380
360
340
320
300
280
260
240
220
200
180
160
140
120
100
80
60
40
20

present

Granodiorite, the O'Briens Creek Supersuite contains the iron–titanium mineral, ilmenite. The occurrence of ilmenite rather than magnetite in the solid granites happened because the molten granite was chemically reduced and thus lacked the oxygen required to form an oxide. These molten rocks also contained an abundance of sulphur-laden gases and were rich in very large atoms such as zirconium, molybdenum, thorium, gold, tungsten, tin, niobium, yttrium and rare earth elements, while they were depleted of small atoms such as fluorine and boron.

Because of the folding, thrusting and melting, the molten rocks that produced the O'Briens Creek Supersuite probably scavenged metals such as thorium and gold from the halo around the older Nundah Granodiorite. This natural recycling of metals is a feature of the Chillagoe district and has occurred many times throughout its long history.

The molten rocks of the O'Briens Creek Supersuite also contained large quantities of steam. As the steam heated up together with the molten rock, it leached potassium, tin, molybdenum, tungsten, copper, gold and fluorine out of the granite. When the granite mass started to solidify, very hot steam rose from it and this steam carried the potassium, tin, molybdenum, tungsten, copper, gold and fluorine in solution. The rising steam expanded and fractured the roof of the granite and the overlying rock. As the steam expanded, it also cooled, became saturated in the dissolved material and precipitated some of the dissolved minerals in fractures. (The same process occurs if large amounts of sugar are dissolved in very hot water. When the super-sweet water is cooled it cannot hold the amount of sugar in solution that the hot water could, and crystals of sugar start to form.)

Thus steam expansion and cooling deposited quartz, molybdenite and gold in the fractures closest to the granite. As the steam continued to move up from the roof of the granite, it continued to expand, cool and fracture the overlying rocks of the Chillagoe Formation. Minerals of tin, copper and fluorine were deposited in the higher fractures. These minerals are the tin oxide cassiterite, the tin–copper–iron sulphide stannite and fluorite, calcium fluoride. In many of the major prospects and mines around the Chillagoe district, such as Red Dome, Harpers and Girofla, tin, molybdenum and fluorine minerals

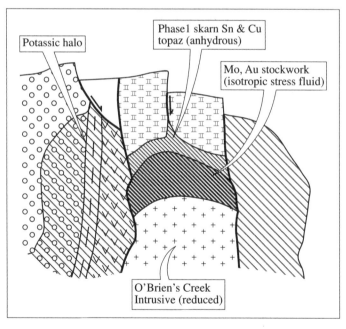

Mineral deposits of molybdenum, gold, tin and copper formed by steam escape from the O'Briens Creek Supersuite granites 325 to 315 million years ago

million years ago
500
480
460
440
420
400
380
360
340
320
300
280
260
240
220
200
180
160
140
120
100
80
60
40
20
present

43

are present that were deposited at this time. It is exceptionally rare in nature to have tin, molybdenum and gold minerals occurring together in the one package of rocks, yet these rare mineral combinations are common in the Chillagoe and Forsayth areas, and are the reason Chillagoe is a jewel box of minerals.

The heat from the O'Briens Creek Supersuite of granites cooked and bleached many of the rocks in the Chillagoe area. Although the mica biotite is normally black, brown biotite developed in the sandstones and siltstones as a result of the clays reacting with iron oxides in these rocks as they were being heated by the granites. Close to limestones, the silty, sedimentary rocks were bleached because hot water pumped through the rocks dissolved some of the dark minerals, converted other dark minerals into light-coloured minerals by chemical reactions with methane, and formed new minerals by materials interchanging between the limestone and siltstone.

In addition, the decomposition of fossil material in the limestone produced gases such as carbon dioxide, methane and hydrogen sulphide. These gases all take part in mineral reactions and, in many cases, are the principal control on the minerals that form. (See colour plates 2, 3, 4 and 5)

Rocks that were originally finely layered siltstones and limestones thus became strongly banded as the result of the heat from the O'Briens Creek Supersuite granites. The bands are defined by layers of hedenbergite, plagioclase, wollastonite, grossular garnet and vesuvianite (calcium–iron–magnesium–aluminium–fluorine silicate). This banding follows the original layering in the limestones, and shows that hot waters containing dissolved materials were moving along, as well as across, layers in the limestone.

The steam from the O'Briens Creek Supersuite also added potassium at high temperatures and pressures. The porphyry dykes were changed to a mixture of pink orthoclase and biotite, whereas the silty and muddy rocks in the Chillagoe area resulted in the formation of mica.

Apart from changing the structure of the rocks themselves, the steam moving up the fractures cooled by expansion and deposited veins of quartz, filling the fractures. These quartz veins contain traces of molybdenite (molybdenum sulphide), scheelite (calcium tungstate) and cassiterite (tin oxide).

The high-temperature, acid, fluorine-rich steam reacted very vigorously with limestone. It took calcium from the limestone, aluminium and silica from the silty sedimentary rocks, and fluorine from the steam, and added carbon dioxide to the steam. Close to the intrusions of the O'Briens Creek Supersuite Granite, such as in the Red Dome open pit, the limestone was changed to a brown, garnet-rich rock composed of the calcium–aluminium silicate mineral grossular garnet with small amounts of the calcium–magnesium–iron silicate (hedenbergite), the calcium–magnesium silicate (diopside), the calcium silicate (wollastonite) and iron oxide (magnetite). The garnets are often zoned, with each layer formed by a new garnet growth around an older garnet crystal. This zoning tells us that the hot waters containing dissolved materials, which enabled garnet growth, were changing in composition over time.

Such changes take place only at high temperatures, when steam-rich fluids add and subtract material to the limestone.

million years ago
500
480
460
440
420
400
380
360
340
320
300
280
260
240
220
200
180
160
140
120
100
80
60
40
20
present

Hydrofluoric acid is used in chemical laboratories to dissolve rock and, in nature, hydrofluoric acid-rich steam at high pressure and high temperature produces the same reaction, and is extremely potent. The major materials added to the limestone at Chillagoe have been iron, aluminium and silica, while carbon dioxide and calcium have been extracted.

Limestone which has been changed by the addition and loss of material is called skarn, an ancient Swedish mining term meaning mullock or waste rock. The conversion of limestone to skarn involves the change from a rock containing low-density minerals (such as calcite) to one with high-density minerals (such as garnet). The increase in density from limestone to skarn results in the formation of large pores between the skarn minerals. These pores are used as pipelines to carry more hot steam into the rock and the pore spaces are later filled up with younger, lower-temperature minerals.

In this way the high-temperature steam added and subtracted material from the limestone which contained small amounts of clays and quartz. These chemical changes formed new minerals in what was originally a slightly dirty limestone. The minerals grossular, hedenbergite and wollastonite were formed by high-temperature reactions, and caused a great decrease in volume (as these are dense minerals). Hot carbon dioxide was also released through fractures as a result of the chemical reactions, rising to the surface in hot springs and gas leaks.

One of the reasons that there is dispute about greenhouse carbon dioxide, and how it can be regulated, is that there is uncertainty about the amount of carbon dioxide that is added to the atmosphere by natural geological processes. The series of well-known mineral reactions that serve to release carbon dioxide into the atmosphere have been duplicated in the laboratory. They are:

limestone + clay + quartz + acid steam = brown garnet (grossular) + carbon dioxide

limestone + quartz + acid steam = wollastonite + carbon dioxide

limestone + quartz + pore water + iron oxide + acid steam = hedenbergite–diopside + carbon dioxide

At a distance from the O'Briens Creek Supersuite granites, the heat of the granite masses was enough to make the very fine-grained calcium carbonate (calcite) in the limestones recrystallise into a coarse-grained marble. However, the heat was not enough to enable mineral reactions to take place and to have the formation of the garnet, wollastonite, diopside or hedenbergite. This coarse-grained recrystallised limestone is the famous Chillagoe marble, which has been quarried at a number of sites near Chillagoe.

Chillagoe marble has many colours. The white is pure coarse-grained calcite, while the pink is composed of coarse-grained calcite with myriads of very fine-grained inclusions of red iron oxides, which impart an overall pink colour to the stone. The blue and black marbles are composed of coarse grains of calcite mixed with decayed biological material, and marble with microscopic-sized fractures smeared with natural oil. Some of the blue marble contains globules of oil within the crystals and other blue marble releases small quantities of

500 — million years ago
480 —
460 —
440 —
420 —
400 —
380 —
360 —
340 —
320 —
300 —
280 —
260 —
240 —
220 —
200 —
180 —
160 —
140 —
120 —
100 —
80 —
60 —
40 —
20 —
present

rotten egg gas (hydrogen sulphide). The rotten egg gas is the sulphurous remains of fossil material in the original limestone: this gas was driven into fractures when the limestone was heated to marble. When the marble is broken, the fractures release hydrogen sulphide.

The heating, cooling and mineral reactions I have described in rocks take many million of years. The cooling process of such large masses of hot rock is aided by water from the surface, too. Percolating cool groundwaters sink down fractures in the hot rocks, the water is heated or even converted to steam, then rises to the surface as hot springs. During cooling, many of the minerals that were stable at high temperature become unstable and react with the circulating cooling water.

The O'Briens Creek Supersuite granites provide evidence of this process. Some of the high-temperature minerals and O'Briens Creek Supersuite rocks contain fractures of low-temperature minerals. These could only have formed after the granites started to be cooled by groundwater circulation. Steam moving up fractures through the limestones leached out some calcium and magnesium. Where these fractures cut through the porphyry dykes, the calcium and magnesium carried by the steam combined with the silica in the porphyry to form hedenbergite. So these hedenbergite veins in the porphyry represent old fractures carrying exhaust steam out of the limestone.

After the garnet-rich rocks and marble formed, steam continued to be released from the cooling masses of granite. Because the garnet-rich rocks formed when the steam was at high pressures and temperatures, they began to become unstable as the steam lost temperature and pressure. The garnet-rich rocks were slightly corroded by the steam, and pink orthoclase feldspar filled in the spaces between the garnet grains. Where the garnet-rich rocks were fractured and steam flowed along the fractures, pink orthoclase feldspar was deposited in the fractures.

The lower temperature and lower pressure pulses of steam carried metals. Not only were the early high-temperature minerals corroded by this steam, but the metal-rich steam became unstable and precipitated metal sulphides in the pores of the rocks. These sulphides are the main ore minerals at Red Dome and other mines in the Chillagoe district, and include the economic copper minerals (bornite and chalcopyrite – copper–iron sulphides; and chalcocite – copper sulphide) in the Red Dome Mine. The steam also carried iron, copper, tin and sulphur, and deposited pyrite (iron sulphide), and rarer minerals such as pyrrhotite (another iron sulphide), stannite (copper–iron–tin sulphide) and tin-rich tetrahedrite (copper–antimony sulphide).

These sulphides were deposited in the garnet-rich rocks as a result of the steam filling the pore spaces and the corrosion of garnet and other minerals. During this last pulse of metal-laden steam, most of the wollastonite in the Red Dome pit formed, new red–brown garnets formed, and the rare minerals ferrobustamite (iron-bearing manganese–calcium silicate) and cuspidine (fluorine-bearing calcium silicate) formed.

The continual passing of steam through the rocks at Chillagoe not only increased the pore spaces in the rocks but physically weakened the rocks. This process can been seen in many experiments and natural environments, the best known being in active earthquake zones. If rocks are under strain and water

500 million years ago
480
460
440
420
400
380
360
340
320
300
280
260
240
220
200
180
160
140
120
100
80
60
40
20
present

is pumped into fault zones, the fault moves and releases energy as an earthquake. At Chillagoe, some of the early high-temperature rocks were weakened by steam and moved, and some of the garnet-rich rocks broke up; garnet grains rolled as a result and became rounded.

Volcanoes at Chillagoe

The volcanic rocks which formed between 325 and 315 million years ago did so in areas where the stress lull had enabled sinking, stretching and breaking of rocks. Volcanoes erupted from numerous local centres, and we now know these as the Pratt Volcanics, Jamtin Volcanics and Redcap Volcanics. As with modern explosive volcanoes, the major material erupted was not lava but ash, which can be thrown out to a high altitude, then fall over a large area, or which can be blasted out of the side of the volcano as a more localised ash flow. Volcanoes also contain debris which has slipped down the steep slopes, sediments deposited in the volcanic lakes and craters, mud flow material derived from the eruption of a crater lake, near-surface intrusions of dykes and plugs, and minor amounts of lava.

The eruption centres at Chillagoe 325 to 315 million years ago were on the continental landmass, and the products were mainly ash falls and ash flows which blanketed very large areas. Lava was rare. Some eruptions threw out clouds of crystals, whereas others hurled very large blocks of solid rock. Some of the ash was reworked and redeposited in the crater by running water. The evidence is that the volcanoes at Chillagoe at this time were therefore little different from modern explosive volcanoes.

The slicing up of Chillagoe

After the granite cooled in the stress lull, and the volcanics had blanketed the surface of the Chillagoe area with ash, geological stresses started to increase again, during the period 315 to 310 million years ago. The tension now, in the compression event called the Alice Springs Orogeny, was in the opposite direction.

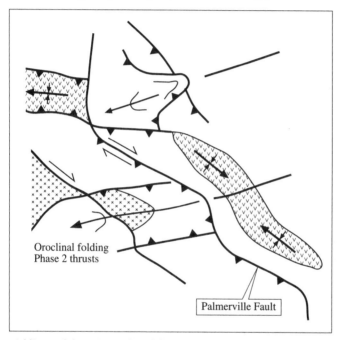

Oroclinal folding
Phase 2 thrusts

Palmerville Fault

Folding and thrusting in the Chillagoe area as a result of the changed stress field

The new compression resulted in the gentle folding of the Redcap, Jamtin and Pratt Volcanics and all the older rocks such as the Chillagoe Formation. The blanketing of the whole of the area by volcanic material meant that, as the rocks were compressed, the volcanics acted like the lid on a pressure cooker. It

million
500 years ago
480
460
440
420
400
380
360
340
320
300
280
260
240
220
200
180
160
140
120
100
80
60
40
20
present

is likely that hot waters were released up fractures and, again, hot springs were active in the Chillagoe area.

Compression reactivated the older faults, such as the Palmerville Fault. This reactivation and movement of faults would have been helped by the hot water held in the pressure-cooked package of rocks. As a result, the Dargalong Metamorphics and Chillagoe Formation were again piled on top of each other as flat slices. (The slicing can be seen today over a wide area of far north Queensland.)

Most of the rock bluffs in the Chillagoe area, especially the Chillagoe limestone, have a near-horizontal system of cracks as a result of this slicing. Such cracks were used by groundwaters to dissolve limestone and form the Chillagoe caves. The flat cracking is seen high in the western wall of the Red Dome pit. However, the flat thrust structures which occur all over far north Queensland as a result of the Alice Springs Orogeny can be seen at their best from the front bar of the Black Cockatoo Hotel! The bleached limestone bluff opposite the hotel has a sequence of almost horizontal subparallel cracks, resulting from the brittle failure of the limestone during the period of major stress 315 to 310 million years ago. (See colour plate 6)

During the Alice Springs Orogeny, the 'lid' of the 'pressure cooker' was broken at some point and fluids were pumped out of the thick pile of rocks at Chillagoe. Compression due to the Orogeny forced rocks up into mountains and the crust of the Earth at Chillagoe was thickened during this mountain-building. As hot waters were pumped up, the water-rich fluids leached gold and minor amounts of copper, lead and zinc from the thick rocks.

These hot metal-rich waters rose, then started to cool and expand and to react chemically with the rocks that they passed through. The metals in solution in the waters became unstable and were precipitated as insoluble gold, copper, lead and zinc minerals. When the hot fluids were pumped up fractures, they also began to expand and cool and, as a result, precipitated chlorite, calcite, gold and copper minerals in quartz veins. Zinc and lead minerals were later precipitated in these quartz veins and the surrounding rocks. This was the second time that the metals in the Chillagoe area had undergone natural recycling. And with each event of recycling, the gold was relocated and reconcentrated. The fluids also reacted with the rocks surrounding the fractures they were rising up. Water was added to minerals in the garnet-rich rocks and minor amounts of amphiboles, chlorite and micas formed.

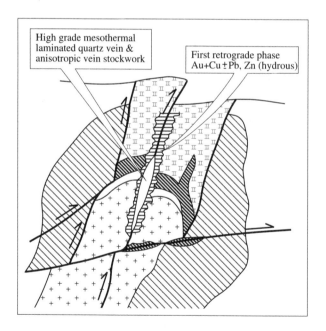

Deposition of gold, copper, lead and zinc minerals in the rocks at Chillagoe during the Alice Springs Orogeny 315 to 310 million years ago

500 million years ago
480
460
440
420
400
380
360
340
320
300
280
260
240
220
200
180
160
140
120
100
80
60
40
20

present

Compression in the Alice Springs Orogeny not only drove water out of the pile of rocks to recycle gold into quartz veins; it also bent some of the rocks in the Red Dome open pit. Layered calcite–magnetite rocks that had formed as a result of the heat and steam released from the O'Briens Creek Supersuite were bent and, in places, broken into blocks of magnetite 'floating' in calcite.

At the time when the Chillagoe area was affected by the Alice Springs Orogeny, the planet was beginning another of its 400-million-year greenhouse/icehouse cycles; Earth was starting to enter an icehouse. (Although we are aware that there are climatic megacycles related to the movement of plates, there is still no adequate explanation for the numerous icehouses and greenhouses during any one of these megacycles.) This icehouse had a profound impact on southern Australia.

With the mountain-building associated with the Alice Springs Orogeny and the rapidly changing climate, flora and fauna, landforms, rainfall and groundwater, it is probable that some of the Chillagoe limestone started to develop, at this time, cave systems that have since been superimposed on and enlarged by later cave-forming events.

More molten rocks and steam

In the Chillagoe area the period 310 to 305 million years ago was one of relaxation between two stressful periods. As previously explained, stress lull, or relaxation, occurs as geological stress is reorienting. A stress lull signals the end of one period of folding or volcanic activity and is the calm before the storm of another period of folding or volcanic activity.

This stress relaxation resulted in the sinking of the crust, the stretching of the sunken portions and the heating of this thinner portion. The heating induced melting of the rocks at depth. The light buoyant melts ascended the sequence at Chillagoe and froze close to the surface as granites (the Almaden and Ootann Supersuites) or erupted as volcanoes (Boonmoo and Nightflower Volcanics). Experiments on the melting of these granites (which crystallise close to the surface) and volcanics (which freeze on the surface) indicate that the buoyant molten material contained very little dissolved water.

Here was the cycle repeating itself. This five-million-year period of melting scavenged from the deep rocks materials that were in the process of melting, and again recycled metals. Furthermore, the molten rock generated at depth rose along fractures and faults generated during the Alice Springs Orogeny. The resultant granites of the Almaden Supersuite have a typical outcrop pattern in the area known as 'metal hills'. These are spectacular hills of angular blocks of bare granite which, in the dry tropics of north Queensland, surprisingly have neither soil cover nor vegetation. Elsewhere in far north Queensland, 'metal hills' are developed on other rock types, such as other types of granites and volcanic rocks, and their development appears to be related to a number of factors.

The weathering pattern that produces 'metal hills' occurs in rocks that are massive, unjointed and silica-rich – in the Chillagoe area, rocks that are associated only with the Almaden Supersuite granites. Furthermore, 'metal hills' occur in situations

million years ago
500
480
460
440
420
400
380
360
340
320
300
280
260
240
220
200
180
160
140
120
100
80
60
40
20
present

with high topographic relief. These areas are exposed to monsoonal rains and strong wind. The products of weathering, which would normally accumulate to form soil, are removed to areas of lower altitude by runoff water during the wet season and the outcrop remains bare. The absence of soil also means there is no adhering vegetation and this further allows rapid seasonal removal of the weathering products. The Almaden Supersuite rocks underwent very rapid weathering and the rate of removal of weathered material exceeded any accumulation of soil. (See colour plate 7)

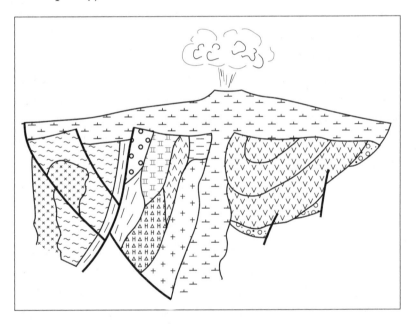

Schematic regional section of the Chillagoe area 310 to 305 million years ago

As the granites of the Almaden and Ootan Supersuites started to cool, the tiny amount of dissolved water contained in the molten rock was released as superheated high-pressure acid steam. The very potent steam leached copper, zinc, lead, silver, gold and arsenic from the granites. The steam was so potent that it also started to corrode the garnet-rich rocks and the porphyry. As the steam rose it expanded and, as a result, it also cooled because it had taken energy from itself to expand. Expansion of steam again fractured the rocks and reactivated earlier fractures.

As the acid steam reacted with the rocks, some minerals were dissolved and new minerals were precipitated. The continual changing of temperature, pressure and chemistry of the steam were such that materials in solution in the steam became unstable and precipitated as new minerals in the rocks. At this time a mixture of pale-green andradite garnet (calcium–iron silicate) with magnetite (iron oxide), bornite (copper–iron sulphide) and chalcocite (copper sulphide) was deposited.

A whole host of rare minerals also formed during this period because the hot high-pressure steam was very complex and contained a great diversity of chemicals. The rare bismuth minerals aikinite, tetradymite, emplectite and joseite have been identified under the microscope, as have more common bismuth minerals such as bismuth and bismuthinite. Numerous arsenic and antimony minerals have also been observed – stibnite, meneghinite, cobaltite, arsenopyrite, glaucodot and tennantite. Rare tellurium minerals, such as native tellurium, hessite, altaite, rickardite and tellurobismutite have been seen under the microscope, too. A few of these minerals (for example, stibnite, antimony sulphide) are present in specimens sufficiently large to be in collections of Chillagoe minerals.

million
500 years ago
480
460
440
420
400
380
360
340
320
300
280
260
240
220
200
180
160
140
120
100
80
60
40
20

present

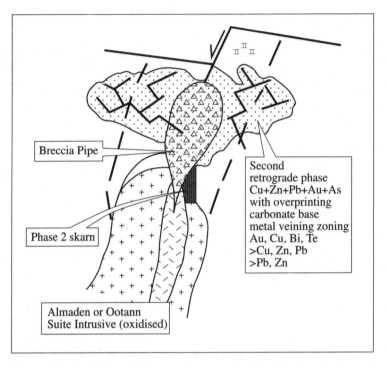

Breccia Pipe

Second
retrograde phase
Cu+Zn+Pb+Au+As
with overprinting
carbonate base
metal veining zoning
Au, Cu, Bi, Te
>Cu, Zn, Pb
>Pb, Zn

Phase 2 skarn

Almaden or Ootann
Suite Intrusive (oxidised)

Mineral deposit formation during the period 310 to 305 million years ago

Some of the horizontal cracks formed during the Alice Springs Orogeny were forced open in the lull. They carried superheated, high-pressure steam which reacted with the rocks around the cracks. In the Red Dome Mine, the cracks carried large amounts of oxygen-rich waters which precipitated a green garnet (the calcium–iron–aluminium silicate, andradite). The presence of minerals such as andradite and magnetite show that the steam released from the Almaden and Ootann Super-suites contained an abundance of oxygen.

As the metal-rich steam rose from the cooling granites, it started to expand. It firstly fractured the overlying rocks, then exploded in these weakened, fractured rocks because the pressure of the steam was far greater than the weight of the rocks. The explosion blew a hole through the Earth's crust. Cracks extended to the surface and most material dropped back into the blast hole. The explosion allowed the steam to escape very rapidly to the surface through a pipe-shaped mass of broken rock. This type of broken rock is called breccia and one of the scenes of this event is known today as the Red Cap breccia pipe.

In the pipe-like body of broken rock, rounded fragments of the green andradite rock, garnet-rich rock and porphyry are found. These fragments have been carried up from depth and have had all their sharp edges ground off in the process.(See colour plate 8)

Now that there was a blast hole of broken-up fragments of rock, further surges of steam were able to move through with ease. While the granites were being cooled by waters circulating through the fractured rock, the rising, expanding steam also became progressively cooler as it rose along fractures and corroded the early garnet-rich rocks. New iron-rich minerals filled the spaces of the corroded high-temperature minerals and grew on top of them. The process of laying down minerals on top of minerals or changing of the outer surface of existing minerals into new ones as a result of the cycles of steam rising through fractures is called overprinting.

Overprinting is a phenomenon we see a lot of in the Chillagoe field. Geologists have used their understanding of the phenomenon to work out the sequence of events of mineral formation there.

million
500 years ago
480
460
440
420
400
380
360
340
320
300
280
260
240
220
200
180
160
140
120
100
80
60
40
20
present

The garnet-rich rocks in the Red Dome Mine were overprinted by sulphides of copper and iron (chalcopyrite, pyrite) associated with haematite (iron oxide), quartz, actinolite (water-bearing calcium–iron–magnesium–aluminium silicate), epidote (water-bearing calcium–iron–aluminium silicate) and diopside (calcium–magnesium silicate). Minor calcite (calcium carbonate), fluorite (calcium fluoride) and chlorite (water-bearing magnesium–iron–aluminium silicate) were associated with these iron-rich minerals. (See colour plate 9)

Groundwater continued to percolate through the broken rock and was heated by the cooling Almaden and Ootan Super-suite granites. The hot groundwater started to rise to the surface as surges of steam, leaching out metals from the broken rocks. As the groundwater cooled, it redeposited calcite (calcium carbonate), gold, copper, bismuth, tellurium, zinc and lead minerals in fractures.

These last surges of steam carried metals in solution, possibly leached from older metal sulphides. The cooling steam finally deposited copper, zinc, lead, silver and arsenic sulphide minerals in the broken rocks. The earlier garnet-rich rocks, marble, and the minerals iron, copper, tin and sulphur from the O'Briens Creek Supersuite steam deposits were broken and overprinted by new minerals such as chalcopyrite, galena (lead sulphide), sphalerite (zinc sulphide), argentite (silver sulphide), arsenopyrite (iron–arsenic sulphide), pyrite (iron sulphide) and bismuth (joseite, tetradymite) and copper tellurides (rickardite).

After many surges of metal-bearing steam, the geothermal system started to collapse back on itself in the dying stages of cooling. As a result, the older minerals were dissolved and new, more stable minerals precipitated. In some places, older higher-temperature minerals were dissolved and re-precipitated as the same mineral but at a lower temperature. The rare octahedral-shaped cavity-linings of galena, for example, formed by such a process.

The last surges of steam moved up fractures which were filled with bladed calcite, fine-grained muscovite (sericite; water-bearing potassium–aluminium silicate), the clay mineral montmorillonite (water-bearing sodium–calcium–aluminium silicate), fluorite, quartz and the carbonates siderite (iron carbonate), ankerite (iron–calcium, magnesium, manganese carbonate) and rhodochrosite (manganese carbonate).

Uplift and ice

As a result of compression or extension, both uplift or sinking can take place at the same time but in different places. Some uplift and sinking is due to loading. For example, at the height of the last glaciation, 18,000 years ago, Scandinavia was covered by an ice sheet more than 2000 metres thick. Scandinavia sunk. The ice sheets melted 8000 years ago and the land started to rise. It is still rising. As an example of this, the castle at Turku in southern Finland was built in the twelfth century on an isolated island. The island is now connected to the land by a spit eight metres above sea level! The land has risen so quickly in the nineteenth century port of Turku that, rather than walk horizontally onto a boat, a ladder is used to climb

million
500 years ago
480
460
440
420
400
380
360
340
320
300
280
260
240
220
200
180
160
140
120
100
80
60
40
20
present

down onto the decks. To compensate for the modern rise of Scandinavia, the lowlands of Europe (Netherlands and northern Germany) are sinking. Sinking and rising due to ice loading and unloading happen because of the relatively plastic, deeper mantle on which the rigid outer skin of our planet sits.

All over the ancient world we see evidence of land rises and falls. The sinking of Venice and the sunken Lydian cities between Kalkan and Antalya in southern Turkey are graphic examples. Modern Bangkok is sinking at an alarming rate because of loading by buildings, compaction derived from motor vehicle-induced vibration and the extraction of ground-water – all of which combine to compress the sediments beneath the city.

The deep, meandering waterways around the city of Sydney (Broken Bay, Sydney Harbour) are a drowned river system that is the result of the Sydney area sinking after the rise of the Great Dividing Range. Beneath the current sea level are old beaches.

In contrast, the famous port city of Efeses in Turkey, the resting place of the Virgin Mary, is now well inland as a result of the land rising. Indeed, many port cities in the ancient world are now far inland, demonstrating that the rising and falling of land are a very common phenomenon.

As will be obvious from the geological history covered so far, the Chillagoe district has undergone numerous events of uplift and sinking. The minor events – equivalent to those we see in Scandinavia, in the ancient world or around the Sydney area – are not preserved in the geological record. It is only the major events of uplift and sinking at Chillagoe that have left their mark.

When the Almaden and Ootann Supersuites of granites

were completely cool as a result of circulating groundwater, 305 million years ago, the Chillagoe area underwent a major uplift. Because the land was now elevated, the weathering, erosion and groundwater systems became far more active. The limestones that were thus exposed were dissolved by rainwater, and the Chillagoe cave system became more extensive.

During the period 305 to 280 million years ago southern Australia was in the grip of glaciation, with a continental ice sheet covering all the southern states, and eastern Australia

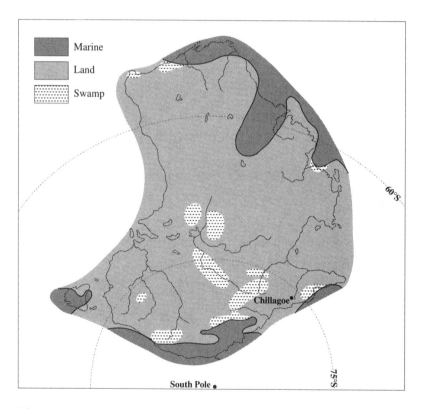

The Australian continent 250 million years ago

underwent alpine glaciation as far north as Rockhampton. Much of Western Australia, central Australia and Queensland was covered by the sea. Continental glaciers disgorged ice into the sea as icebergs, and these dropped boulders onto the sea floor, or the floors of lakes dammed by glacial debris, as they melted. Australia then was still part of the giant supercontinent Gondwana; to the south it was joined to Antarctica and to the west, to India. It was very close to the South Pole. The Chillagoe area at that time was not covered by ice, but its climate became cool, windy and dry.

By contrast, the climate of equatorial Europe was arid. Large red dunes, salt pans and shallow seas were present. Much of the salt from the salt mines of the United Kingdom, Germany, Poland and Russia formed during these times, in the Zechstein and Perm Basins.

Stress, molten rocks and explosions

Some time in this dry, glacial era the Chillagoe area underwent yet another period of stress. Diagonal stresses were so strong that the Palmerville Fault moved again, and was re-oriented into its present north-western direction.

At Chillagoe, diagonal stresses forced the crust to stretch and thin, resulting in the formation of north–south rifts. The thin crust over the Earth's hot mantle in these rifts began to melt and, because these melts were light, to move upwards in fractures. Some of the melts solidified in fractures as dykes, others spread out as horizontal layers, and others formed larger pods of granite. As we can see from the long history of the Chillagoe area, the breaking up of the crust (stretching) and the stitching together of the bits of crust (compression) have never ceased over the passage of time.

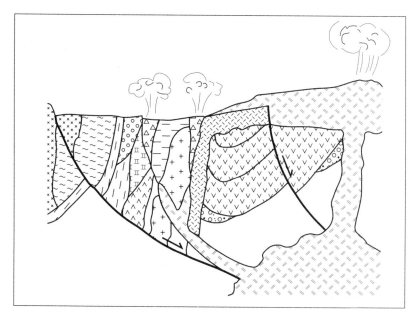

Volcanoes and granites in the Chillagoe area, 305 to 280 million years ago

The solidification of the first molten rocks from this event, called the Lags Supersuite, baked the rocks in the Chillagoe district and sealed up fractures and pores. After the first small volumes of molten rock pushed their way up, steam was released from the cooling granites. The steam was trapped in the rocks because the fractures and pores had been sealed, and pressure began to rise.

million
years ago

500
480
460
440
420
400
380
360
340
320
300
280
260
240
220
200
180
160
140
120
100
80
60
40
20

present

Eventually the pressure of the superheated steam was so great that the steam exploded through to the surface. Rock fragments were blasted out of the explosion craters, other rock fragments fell down the blast holes and gas streamed out of the pipes of broken rock. The remains of such pipes can be seen in the Chillagoe area at Red Dome, Harpers, Mungana, Morrisons, Wilson's Line and Arachnid, as well as Red Cap.

After the explosion, the rise of hot acid fluids resulted in the precipitation of iron sulphides, chalcopyrite, galena, sphalerite, arsenic and antimony minerals. As the geothermal system started to cool, it recharged, and heated groundwater circulated through the broken rock, cooling and leaching metals from them. The copper sulphide chalcocite was then deposited in the broken rock. The last and lowest temperature stage of groundwater circulation leached out copper and redeposited native copper and calcite in veins. This is a rare feature in nature because, in hot fluids, copper normally combines with sulphur to form sulphides. Large amounts of calcite were stripped from the Chillagoe limestone and redeposited as calcite during the closing stages of this geothermal event. Some calcite contained traces of manganese, which imparted a pink colour, whereas other calcite was coloured orange–brown by admixtures of iron.

The flushing of large amounts of fluid through the pile of rocks created space. As the Lags Supersuite continued to be cooled by the circulating groundwaters, the geothermal system started to die. Only warm water was able to be pumped through fractures and pores. The later waters precipitated minerals which lined these spaces with calcite, arsenopyrite and pyrite. In places, amethystine quartz overprinted the arsenopyrite.

Other calcite-rich veins contain crystals of the antimony sulphide stibnite.

The stream of hot, acid steam rising up through the pipe of broken rock mixed with descending cool groundwaters to form a diversity of materials, jasper being the most common. (The rock jasper is composed of silica precipitated from steam, hot springs or boiling water. It is red–brown due to minor amounts of iron oxides, and is invariably enriched by the elements which typically surround hot springs, such as arsenic, antimony, sulphur, mercury, silver and gold.) The minerals alunite (water-bearing potassium–aluminium sulphate), dickite (water-bearing aluminium silicate), adularia (potassium–aluminium silicate) and marcasite (iron sulphide) have also been found in the pipe of broken rock. In modern geothermal settings, these minerals form only from hot, extremely acid steam or water, and such observations have been duplicated in the laboratory by making minerals.

In addition, minor amounts of the iron oxide haematite have formed in the pipes of broken rock. Haematite is an oxygen-rich mineral and its presence shows that the hot acid steam, hot springs and boiling water were very rich in oxygen. This oxygen was probably introduced into the system by the sinking into the hot spring recharge area of cool surface water containing dissolved air. The haematite imparts a reddish-brown colour to the broken rock in the pipes. Calcium fluoride (fluorite) is also present in some of the pipes of broken rock. The calcium derives from the leaching of large quantities of fractured and altered limestone, whereas the fluorine is derived from acid waters released from the Lags Supersuite granites.

million
500 years ago
480
460
440
420
400
380
360
340
320
300
280
260
240
220
200
180
160
140
120
100
80
60
40
20
present

Because calcium fluoride (fluorite) is highly insoluble, the mixing of calcium-rich waters with acid fluorine-rich waters would have resulted in the sudden precipitation of fluorite.

We can deduce that, in the Chillagoe area 280 million years ago, hot springs bubbled out on the surface, boiling mud pools were widespread and steam geysers were active. (The area would have been little different from modern active geothermal areas such as Rotorua in New Zealand.) The extremely acid waters for the hot springs and steam vents rose along faults and fractures. As the mineral-laden steam expanded, cooled and mixed with surface waters, fluorite was being deposited in the faults and fractures. Experiments and observations on the behaviour of active geothermal systems show that silica precipitates when the temperature of the hot fluids decreases, so the mixing of rising hot steam with descending cool groundwaters would have induced the precipitation of silica as well as the fluorite.

Mixing of these two types of fluids took place in fractures. The fractures were sealed by the precipitated silica and, because the steam could no longer escape, the pressure of the steam would have increased until it was so great that it broke the fracture. More steam was released along the faults and fractures, only to expand, cool and precipitate more silica. Again, the fractures were sealed and again the steam pressure rose and broke the silica, filling the faults and fractures. This process, called crack-seal, has taken place hundreds of times at Chillagoe to produce laminated quartz veins. Many of these laminated quartz-adularia veins are exceptionally rich in gold; others in the Chillagoe district have been mined for fluorite.

Hot springs in modern settings form terraces of silica-rich material called sinter. Sinter terraces are commonly draped down the slopes of hills. Underneath the cold sinter terraces at Chillagoe, crystals of calcite and sulphates such as baryte (barium sulphate) were being deposited in the pipes of broken rock. These were later replaced by silica and the replacement was so perfect that the tabular and radial shape of the crystals is still preserved. The replacement process involves the leaching out of the original components of the minerals and the filling of the space by a new mineral. In some of these veins beneath the sinters, tabular crystals of carbonate and sulphate minerals were formed in openings left in the faults and fractures which acted as the hot spring upflow zones. During crack-seal, these minerals have been totally replaced by silica.

Links to Mars

The silica sinter and red hematite precipitated at the surface by the hot acid steam are still present in the Chillagoe area, having been draped down the sides of hills 290 million years ago as mineral-laden steam erupting at the surface in the form of geysers and hot springs. We know that boiling mud pools were also present. And evidence of a fine-grained, layered, brownish mud with gas bubble escape structures, found at Griffiths Hill and Harpers in the Chillagoe area, shows a distinct similarity to the mud in the modern geysers, hot springs and boiling mud pools in New Zealand.

Hot springs are of great interest to scientists, not only for an understanding of geothermal activity, but for the life that they contain. Modern hot springs – smokers – in places such as Rotorua, and Yellowstone National Park in the United States,

500 million years ago
480
460
440
420
400
380
360
340
320
300
280
260
240
220
200
180
160
140
120
100
80
60
40
20
present

contain a great diversity of the microbiological organisms known as thermophilic bacteria which, as we have seen, live in high-temperature, extremely acid waters and derive energy from the heat of the water, not from sunlight. The waters that support such life contain very high levels of material toxic to humans such as arsenic, mercury and antimony.

Hot-spring biota has been observed associated with mid-ocean ridge submarine hot springs at depths of three kilometres. Here, life thrives in the dark and at high pressures. Some organisms derive their nutrients from black smokers of super-heated acid water at 250 to 420 degrees Celsius. This water contains myriads of particles of metal sulphides, sulphates and oxides. Other micro-organisms live around the cooler white smokers and extract oxygen from the sulphate exhaled by these.

It is quite possible that life first evolved independently as micro-organisms in hot springs on both Earth and Mars. Other less likely possibilities are that thermophilic life could have been carried from Mars to Earth by a Martian meteorite, or that life could have been carried from Earth to Mars by a terrestrial meteorite. (The recent discovery of fossil bacteria in a Martian meteorite makes this within the bounds of possibility. If we go back to the dawn of time, humans may be genetically related to life on Mars!)

Mars once had very large, active volcanoes with which we would expect hot springs, geysers and boiling mud pools to be associated. It also once had running surface water, which formed giant meandering river systems, deep ravines and alluvial fans; but this is now all gone. The early history of Mars was therefore like that of Earth, and it is probable that life also independently evolved on Mars but was rendered extinct by the loss of running water. Any ancient life on Mars is most likely to have been preserved as microbiological fossils in hot spring sinters, very similar to those at Chillagoe. (See colour plates 10, 11 and 12)

Collapse of the hot springs

As the heat source for a geothermal system is cooled by circulating groundwaters, the fractures used for the ascent of steam are also used for the descent of cool groundwater. The fractures have a zonation of minerals with depth, which is a reflection of the changes in temperature, acidity, concentration and pressure of the geothermal fluids. Just to make matters complicated, superimposed upon these zoned minerals are another set of zoned minerals – those formed by the descending groundwaters.

At Chillagoe, deep down in the pipes of broken rock, the steam had leached metals from the fractured rocks, and chlorite, kaolinite and carbonate minerals filled the spaces between the fragments of rock, replacing some of them. The serpentine-like water-bearing iron–aluminium silicate bertherine was formed by the reaction of acid-oxidised steam with the silicate minerals. Kaolinite is a very common mineral, most frequently found in soils as a result of weathering, when it has a very disordered mineral structure and its extremely small platey layers are bent, separated and of variable thickness. In contrast to kaolinite formed during weathering, the kaolinite from the pipes of broken rock, such as those at Mungana, is a highly ordered crystalline mineral. The ordering of its atoms is expressed in the hand speci-

million years ago
500
480
460
440
420
400
380
360
340
320
300
280
260
240
220
200
180
160
140
120
100
80
60
40
20
present

mens of this type of kaolinite, which are waxy, with a high sheen.

Further up the pipe of broken rock, the metal-rich steam redeposited metal sulphides, a potassium feldspar (adularia), clay minerals (kaolinite again, illite) and large quantities of silica. Minerals like adularia have a story to tell. In laboratory experiments and in geothermal systems, adularia forms only from low-temperature, low-pressure, acid waters – so its presence gives us clues about the old geothermal systems at Chillagoe.

The pipes of broken rock were up to one kilometre in diameter. They underwent a number of steam explosions, material

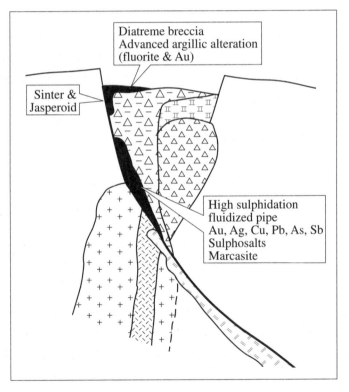

Deposition of gold, base metals and fluorite between 305 and 280 million years ago

being blasted out of the pipes into the atmosphere. Pieces of the surface sinter fell down into the pipe of broken rock and were cemented there by minerals precipitated from the cooling steam.

The continual rise of very acid steam up the pipes of broken rock resulted in the precipitation of minerals between the fragments in the pipe and the corrosion of some of the minerals formed in earlier episodes. Minerals of gold, silver, copper, lead, arsenic and antimony were deposited in the pipes of broken rock as well as the minerals characteristic of extremely acid, relatively low-temperature conditions such as alunite, dickite, adularia and marcasite.

After the peak of the geothermal system, about 290 million years ago, cooler waters collapsed back into the pile of broken rock. The water reacted with hot rock to form clay minerals such as kaolinite, illite, montmorillonite and vermiculite. Then the descending oxidised waters reacted with chlorite. The iron in the chlorite was converted to haematite and the magnesium, aluminium and silicate precipitated as more clay minerals. Oxidation of sulphides and reaction by the hot water with limestone or calc-silicate minerals formed the water-bearing calcium sulphate gypsum. Hot sulphides were attacked by the descending, cooler oxidised waters, large volumes of sulphuric acid were released and this alteration prepared the ground for weathering.

Because the rocks were intensely fractured and metal sulphides were now close to the surface, rainwater would have percolated through the metal sulphide-rich mineral deposits such as Red Dome. At that time, the climate was cool and dry and dissolved air in the rainwater would have oxidised some of

million years ago

500
480
460
440
420
400
380
360
340
320
300
280
260
240
220
200
180
160
140
120
100
80
60
40
20

present

the sulphides in the upper levels of the Red Dome and other ore deposits in the district.

The oxygen-rich rainwater would also have slightly oxidised the copper minerals bornite, chalcocite and chalcopyrite. Sooty bluish–black covellite (copper sulphide) formed immediately below the water table and native copper formed at the water table. Although pure native copper is metallic, the natural native copper is coated with black-to-brown copper oxides or green copper carbonate (malachite). There was a minor concentration of gold, too, as the acid oxygen-rich groundwaters dissolved gold, moved it deeper and re-precipitated it in a concentrated zone at the water table.

Higher above the water table, copper carbonates, such as the blue azurite and green malachite, formed. With intense weathering the copper silicate chrysocolla may have formed above the water table at that time. When percolating acid groundwaters meet feldspars or micas, sodium, potassium and calcium are stripped from these minerals into the water. Clay is left behind as the product of intense acid weathering, which might explain some of the clays at Chillagoe.

The cool rainwater would have dissolved large quantities of limestone, resulting in the enlargement of the Chillagoe cave system. In contrast to most other materials, limestone is highly soluble at low temperature and only slightly soluble in warmer conditions.

Massive volcanic eruptions

One of the biggest volcanic eruptions ever to occur on Earth happened in far north Queensland around 280 million years ago, when some 2000 cubic kilometres of material erupted from the Featherbed Volcano, located to the northeast of Chillagoe. By contrast, the 1981 eruption of Mount St Helens in Washington State, USA – which received enormous publicity – erupted 1.3 cubic kilometres of material.

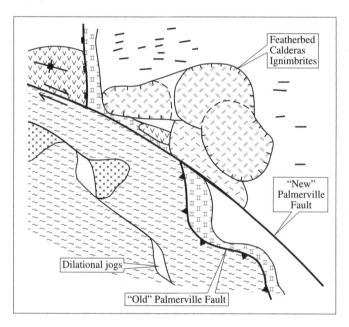

Volcanic centres around Chillagoe 305 to 280 million years ago

The Featherbed Volcanics erupted from a series of eight distinct volcanic centres over an area 100 kilometres long by 30 kilometres wide. The centres of eruption were in a north-westerly

500 million years ago
480
460
440
420
400
380
360
340
320
300
280
260
240
220
200
180
160
140
120
100
80
60
40
20
present

direction parallel to the Palmerville Fault. The rising molten rock for the eruptions used fractures associated with the fault to get to the surface, and exploited a major crustal weakness parallel to it. Such weaknesses exist for a very long time on Earth and are continually reactivated and exploited by molten rocks and fluids.

The Featherbed eruption was highly explosive. Quartz-rich molten rocks rose from great depth and, near the surface, a large amount of water dissolved in them. As the water-rich molten rocks rose the last three kilometres through the crust to the surface, the water pressure in the rock became far higher than the pressure of the overlying rocks. The quartz-rich melt became overpressurised, the overlying rocks failed and, with a decrease in the weight of the overlying rocks, the dissolved steam was catastrophically released from the molten rock.

The massive steam-driven explosion blasted out the rocks as fragments. These were mixed with crystals which had started to form in the quartz-rich melt, superheated gas (mainly steam) released when the overburden was blasted off, and the molten rock itself. But there wasn't just one eruption: numerous explosions from the Featherbed Volcano left behind huge craters.

The superheated blast material flowed great distances across the land surface, even uphill, at speeds of up to 200 kilometres per hour, flattening everything in its wake. When it settled, it heated up and all the fragments fused with each other to form a rock called ignimbrite. This was the largest volume of material erupted from the Featherbed Volcano.

We have evidence of numerous massive ignimbrite eruptions, which blanketed the area many times; there were also local minor lava and ash eruptions. Most of the Chillagoe area was covered by ignimbrite. The pipes of broken rock formed by the explosions of the Lags Supersuite were covered and preserved by the ignimbrites of the Featherbed Volcanics. The volcanics themselves were subsequently covered by sedimentary rocks, which have since been removed, and the present skyline of the Chillagoe area is the old land surface of 280 million years ago. The ignimbrite of the Featherbed Volcanics is rugged, steeply incised and hilly country.

There are many modern volcanoes similar to the ancient Featherbed Volcano. These occur in the Mediterranean (for instance, Santorini), across Asia (Tambora, Indonesia) and in belts around the Pacific Ocean (Mount Fuji, Japan). The modern Taupo Volcanic Zone of New Zealand is very similar also. Although ignimbrite is one of the major products erupting from modern volcanoes, the explosive emulsion of gas-melt-solid which forms ignimbrite is, for obvious reasons, only observed very rarely. Ignimbrite eruptions are lethal and only one person is known to have survived a modern ignimbrite eruption.

Lava eruptions from quartz-rich melts have been very rare in both modern and ancient events. Normally the molten rock either freezes solid beneath the surface or explodes. The frozen lava forms domes and sheets which have a long history of being cooled by circulating groundwaters. Areas of cooling lava domes have hot springs, geysers, gas explosion craters, sinters and boiling mud pools. The traditional view of Hell with fire and brimstone (sulphur) derives from Dante, who observed (at the Lardarello geothermal field in Italy) explosion craters lined

500 — million years ago
480
460
440
420
400
380
360
340
320
300
280
260
240
220
200
180
160
140
120
100
80
60
40
20

present

with sulphur crystals, steam vents releasing rotten egg gas and sulphur dioxide, and hot rocks. Such cooling lava domes provide the steam for geothermal power stations in Italy and New Zealand.

On the other hand, ash falls from modern quartz-rich volcanoes are very common (one occurred recently in the Philippines) and can have devastating results for all life. Numerous deaths can result from asphyxiation by the ash, as was the case at Pompeii. Fine particles of ash in the atmosphere create friction and electrical currents, and lightning flashes often coincide. The fine particles nucleate water vapour, and deluges often occur after eruptions. The rain and resultant flooding shift ash off slopes, create landslides and result in ash-clogged flooded rivers. Furthermore, thick layers of ash lying on buildings result in the collapse of roofs, with inevitable human fatalities.

Ash eruptions have also been known to have less tragic consequences. In a recent Indonesian eruption, a Boeing 747 flew through the stratospheric ash cloud, and its jet engines were choked by it. Three of the four engines stalled and the plane went into a dive. But when it reached ash-free, thicker air at lower altitude, its engines restarted. However, the engines were irreparably scoured by the abrasive ash. Spectacular sunsets occur after ash eruptions, because the fine particles take more than a year to settle from the upper atmosphere. These particles reflect sunlight and there are numerous historical records of cooler, wetter, global climates in the few years following a major ash eruption.

Then there are the hazards of old volcanic craters, which often fill with water. Muddy and sandy sediments are deposited in the craters and, because these structures are usually steep-sided, landslide material falls into them. If such craters are reactivated, the water, mud, sand and boulders lying in them are blasted out as a mud flow. Mud flows contain superheated steam, flow both downhill and uphill at speeds of more than 100 kilometres per hour, and are lethal for valley populations – even those living a great distance from an eruption. Tens of thousands of people were killed by the mud flows from the 1815 Tambora eruption in Indonesia.

When an eruption takes place beneath an ice sheet (for instance, in Iceland and at Mount St Helens, USA), much of the ice melts. The boundary between ice and the underlying rock becomes steamy, propelling huge masses of ice many cubic kilometres in size rapidly across the land surface. The melting ice produces mud flows, landslides and flooding.

The eruption of volcanic islands brings forth the lethal mix of hot molten rock and water. In 1883, the eruption of the island of Krakatoa in Indonesia was so great that most of the island (and its population) was blasted into the atmosphere. The tidal wave that resulted was measured in Cape Town and the sonic boom was heard in Perth! The mythical Atlantis was probably the Greek island of Thira (Santorini). The myth suggests that Atlantis and its population disappeared and there is much evidence to support this in Santorini. Minoan houses excavated there look as if there was a rapid departure, as normal household items remain and only the valuables have been removed. It is probable that the Minoans of Santorini took to the sea following a major eruption, only to be killed by either the sonic boom or the tidal waves. An ash layer covers the

million
500 years ago
480
460
440
420
400
380
360
340
320
300
280
260
240
220
200
180
160
140
120
100
80
60
40
20

present

Cycladean islands (for example, Milos, Kimolos, Santorini) which would have asphyxiated the inhabitants there, whereas the coastal-dwelling Minoans of Crete would have been destroyed by the tidal waves.

But the biggest killer resulting from modern (and presumably historical) quartz-rich volcanoes is starvation. Eruptions decimate crops, water is polluted, livestock are killed and all infrastructure is destroyed. If a volcano the size of the ancient Featherbed Volcano erupted again today, hundreds of thousands to millions of human casualties would be expected. (See colour plate 13)

Cool climates and coal

During the era of the eruption of the Featherbed Volcanics – about 280 million years ago – Australia was still experiencing a cool climate. Large coal basins were forming, from southern New South Wales to central Queensland, as were small basins in Western Australia and Tasmania. These coal basins formed because much of eastern Australia was undergoing compression to form a volcanic island arc (for example, the New England district of New South Wales and Queensland). In the hinterland behind the arc, eastern Australia was stretched and rifted; and, as a result large, subsiding basins started to form.

At the same time, far north Queensland experienced very weak diagonal stresses which resulted in slight stretching, rifting and the development of lowlands. Small basins formed and faults developed at the edge of these. Sediments were washed from the surrounding highlands into the basins and, as they

Plate 1:
Discontinuous ridges of
fossiliferous limestones of the
Chillagoe Formation between
the Red Dome Mine and Mungana.

Plate 2: (top left)
Grossular garnet
crystals, Red Dome
open pit.

Plate 3: (top right)
Garnet-bornite skarn,
Red Dome open pit.

Plate 4: (bottom left)
Banded magnetite-
calcite-chalcopyrite rock,
Red Dome open pit.

Plate 5: (bottom right)
Veining of porphyry by
numerous generations of
quartz and hedenbergite,
Red Dome open pit.

Plate 6: (top)
Flat thrust structures in
the Chillagoe Limestone
formed during the Alice
Springs Orogeny 315 to
310 million years ago.

Plate 7: (bottom)
The 'metal hills' of
Chillagoe, composed
of Almaden Supersuite
granite 325 to 315
million years old.

Plate 8: (top)
Red Cap matrix-
supported breccia
showing a diversity
of fragments.

Plate 9: (bottom)
Calcite crystals
deposited in a cavity.

Plate 10: (top)
Silicified siltstone which
was originally a boiling
mud pool. Gas columns
are still preserved.

Plate 11: (bottom)
Layered silica sinter left
at the surface as a result
of geysers, hot springs
and boiling mineral-laden
water during modern
volcanicity.

Plate 12: (top)
Coloured masses of hot
spring microbiological
life thriving in the hot
acid metal-rich boiling
pools at Rotorua,
New Zealand.

Plate 13: (bottom)
Jointed ignimbrite from
the Featherbed Volcanics
cauldron, Walsh River.

Plate 14: (top)
Isolated pinnacle of
weathered limestone,
Red Dome.

Plate 15: (bottom)
Malachite-stained
gossan, Griffiths Hill.

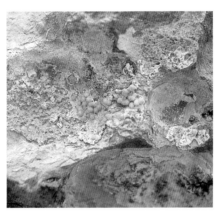

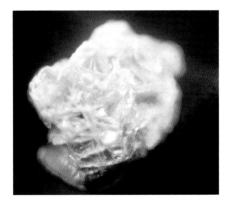

Plate 16: (top)
Laminated calcite-
aurichalcite,
Penzance Mine.

Plate 17: (middle)
Conichalcite and
chrysocolla, Red
Dome open pit.

Plate 18: (bottom)
'Chillagite',
Christmas Gift Mine.

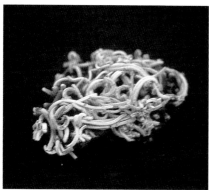

Plate 19: (top)
Overgrowth of calcite
on malachite, Red
Dome open pit.

Plate 20: (bottom)
Malachite pseudomorph
of wire copper,
Red Dome open pit.

Plate 21: (top)
Overgrowth and
partial pseudomorph
of azurite by cerussite,
Eclipse Mine.

Plate 22: (bottom)
Calcite-lined cavity
overprinted by striated
azurite, Red Dome
open pit.

Plate 23: (top)
Anglesite crystals on
iron oxides, Christmas
Gift Mine.

Plate 24: (bottom)
Cuprite, Red
Dome open pit.

Plate 25: (top)
Cuprite and native
copper, Red Dome
open pit.

Plate 26: (middle)
'Chalcotrichtite',
Christmas Gift Mine.

Plate 27: (bottom)
Partial replacement of
native copper by cuprite
which in turn is replaced
by malachite, Red Dome
open pit.

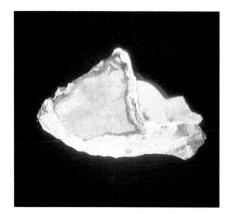

Plate 28: (top)
Reaction zone of cuprite
between red cuprite and
green malachite, Red
dome open pit.

Plate 29: (middle)
Ruby red cuprite,
Red Dome open pit.

Plate 30: (bottom)
Cuprian nontronite,
Red Dome open pit.

Plate 31: (top)
Defunct workings,
Lady Jane Mine.

Plate 32: (bottom)
Open pit and shaft beam
pump, Girofla Mine.

Plate 33: (top)
Aerial shot of the
defunct Chillagoe
smelters.

Plate 34: (bottom)
Ropy slag, Chillagoe.

Plate 35: (top)
Aerial photograph of
Red Dome open pit.

Plate 36: (bottom)
Mungana gold and base
metals-gold prospect.

started to fill with sediments, cool-climate swamps formed. We can tell from the lack of diversity of fossil species and their morphology that the vegetation formed in cool swamps.

Accumulation of decaying plant material in the subsiding swamp allowed the development of peat which, over time, was compressed into coal. As the basin became loaded with sediment, the bounding fault moved, allowing the basin to sink. More sediment was able to pour into the subsided basin and the whole process took place again, producing numerous stacked coal seams. The mountainous Featherbed Volcanics surrounding the small basins allowed fine muds and clays to be washed into the peat, so the final coal that resulted became 'dirty' with a high ash content.

The Mount Mulligan coalfield, north of Dimbulah, was later to provide coal to the smelters at Chillagoe. Here the fossil material from the decaying vegetation found in the coal shows evidence of extensive cool temperate swamps. These were dominated by *Glossopteris* plants that were separated by hills and slopes containing early ginkos and the first conifers. Horsetails, cycad-ancestors, rushes, ferns, seed-ferns and mosses were abundant. *Glossopteris* is a deciduous plant, which is evidence for a cold climate. Additionally, the tree rings of other fossil plants show very close and uniform annual rings, indicating a cold climate when the plants were dormant in winter and had only short growth periods. So we know that the Mount Mulligan coals are dominated by fossils of plants which grew in cold upland swamps at some distance from the sea. The species, examples of typical Gondwana flora, are found also as fossils in India, South Africa, South America and Antarctica.

million years ago

500
480
460
440
420
400
380
360
340
320
300
280
260
240
220
200
180
160
140
120
100
80
60
40
20

present

When one thinks of the formation of peat from decaying vegetable matter, tropical forests and swamps immediately come to mind. However, large tropical swamps – such as the modern Amazon Basin – are not the precursors of coal. The vigorous microbiological activity that occurs in warm conditions ensures that plant material very rapidly decays to water, carbon dioxide and methane. No peat is found in the Amazon Basin. Modern peat is found only at high latitudes (for example, in Patagonia, Ireland, Scotland, Scandinavia, Siberia and Canada) where the cold has slowed microbiological activity. Modern peat forms in all vegetated high-latitude environments, from coastal swamps to uplands. Peat is commonly associated with glacial gravels and it is no surprise that coal is also associated with rocks of glacial origin.

Crisis in life

During the deposition of the sands, silts and peat in the land-locked basin at Mount Mulligan, profound changes were occurring in the oceans. There was a great crisis in the history of life on Earth 245 million years ago. At this time, 96 per cent of all species on the planet became extinct. Mysteriously, almost no terrestrial plants or animals became extinct, while almost all shallow marine animals suddenly disappeared. Such mass extinctions have a profound effect on the history of life on Earth.

The reason for this, the greatest mass extinction that Earth has experienced, is unknown. Of the five great mass extinctions (approximately 430, 368, 245, 208 and 65 million years ago), three can be attributed to meteorites or comets striking Earth – those of 368, 208 and 65 million years ago. Massive impact craters of these ages have been found. When a huge meteorite or comet some ten kilometres in diameter hits the planet, it does so at a huge velocity, and large amounts of dust are thrown into the atmosphere from the impact crater, which is generally more than fifty kilometres wide. A massive impact also triggers volcanism, which ejects more dust and gases into the atmosphere.

With an atmosphere full of dust, sunlight cannot penetrate effectively to the ground, the atmosphere cools and plant and animal life starts to perish. Furthermore, the impact debris heats the atmosphere when it falls back to Earth and species are cooked to extinction. The rapid collapse of the food chain is like a snowball, and more and more life dies during the mass extinction until the atmosphere reverts to its pre-impact state.

But the greatest mass extinction of all time, 245 million years ago, is not associated with a known major meteorite impact. There is no evidence of a massive change in climate or sea level at that time. So what triggered it? One possibility is that a nearby star the size of our Sun was compressed to a sphere ten kilometres across, becoming first a supernova and then a neutron star. A supernova explosion would have bombarded the Earth with 100,000 years worth of cosmic energy in a day. If these rays had hit the upper atmosphere, a shower of high energy particles (muons) would have rained down on Earth. Such a particle bombardment would have killed both plants and animals directly through radiation, as well as destroying the ozone layer and making the environment radioactive. However, although

500 — million years ago
480
460
440
420
400
380
360
340
320
300
280
260
240
220
200
180
160
140
120
100
80
60
40
20

present

spectacularly catastrophic, evidence is against this theory, as land plants were unaffected.

There is some evidence of massive Siberian volcanic eruptions at this time. One suggestion is that sulphurous gas released from such eruptions killed life on Earth. However, as the land plants did not become extinct this process appears unlikely. The mass extinction primarily affected animal life in the oceans and may well have been due to a global disease pandemic. Some viruses today are known to affect more than one

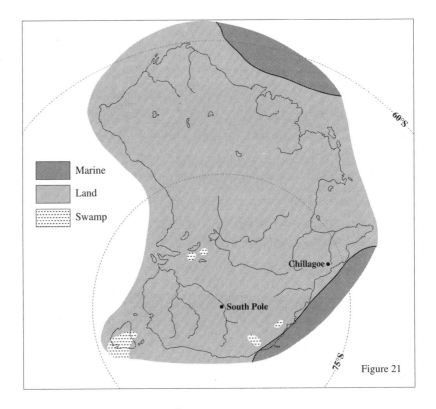

Figure 21

The Australian continent 220 million years ago

species (for example, AIDS, mad cow disease/Creutzfeldt-Jakob disease) and this, to date, is the best explanation we have for the biggest mass extinction recorded.

When this crisis occurred, Australia was still at high latitudes in the southern hemisphere – that is, close to the South Pole. The continental land mass had stopped rotating clockwise and had started to rotate anti-clockwise instead.

Warping

The next major geological change took place 260 million years ago and again at 240 to 220 million years ago. Much of eastern Australia was compressed in the Hunter-Bowen Orogeny. The Hunter Valley and Bowen Basin coalfields were gently warped, major faults moved and the rocks in the small coal basin at Mount Mulligan were gently warped. The Palmerville Fault probably moved again.

At about 208 million years ago, there was another mass extinction of life, when a huge meteorite hit Earth and left a 100-kilometre-wide crater in Manicouagan, Quebec, Canada. There was a quick filling of vacant ecological niches by rapidly evolving life, and this sudden change in life determined the boundary between the Triassic and Jurassic geological periods. It is not known whether the warping at the time was triggered by, or has an indirect relationship to, the massive meteorite impact.

500 million years ago
480
460
440
420
400
380
360
340
320
300
280
260
240
220
200
180
160
140
120
100
80
60
40
20
present

Extraterrestrial influence

Although we know that the impact of meteorites causes global mass extinctions of life, we really do not know what is happening on the other side of the planet as a result of the meteorite hit. We have evidence from the Deccan basalts in India that an impact in the Gulf of Mexico 65 million years ago triggered massive volcanism. In eastern Australia, including Chillagoe, a stress reversal and compression began 370 million years ago, and this is when the meteorites that are correlated with global extinctions of life hit Sweden and Canada.

The massive eruptions of the Featherbed Volcano some 280 million years ago are enigmatic because these are among the largest known eruptions on the planet. It is possible that meteorite impacting on the other side of the planet triggered this volcanism at Chillagoe. There are two Canadian meteorite impact craters, at Clearwater, of thirty-two and twenty-two kilometres in diameter, which are poorly dated at 290 million years plus or minus 20 million years. Although the uncertainty of the timing of this impact is large, we have greater certainty that a minor mass extinction took place 290 million years ago at the end of the geological time period known as the Carboniferous.

There have been more than twenty minor mass extinctions, some of which can be correlated with meteorite impact craters of at least 32 kilometres in diameter. Most minor mass extinctions are used as the boundaries between two geological periods, because the vacant ecologies were filled very quickly with new species and so fossils can be dated accurately. The fossil record is not just a record of the evolution of life and the ancient environments in which it thrived; it is also a record of the numerous events of life.

There are some mass extinctions which cannot be related to known impact sites, and some craters greater than 32 kilometres in diameter cannot be related to a mass extinction. One example is the 55-kilometre-wide Tookoonooka crater in Queensland, dated at 128 million years old. The answer may lie in dating problems. The timing of the Tookoonooka meteorite hit may be inaccurate, while the timing of the minor mass extinction at the end of the Jurassic period has been variably dated over the last decade in the range 130 to 145.6 million years ago. As with much science, more measurement and re-measurement is needed, to see whether the two events can be linked. Work such as this constitutes part of the exciting, unfinished business of science.

In the Gulf of Mexico, the crater from the latest impact-induced major mass extinction, 65 million years ago, is filled with sediment, but its shape can be mapped by detailed measurement of the magnetic field, the Earth's gravity and earthquake shock waves over the impact site. The occurrence of meteorite debris in material 65 million years old is well-documented. For example, there is a clay horizon which contains iridium-rich clay (which was once dust covering the planet), small pieces of meteorite material, glass fragments (from molten rock blasted from the impact site into the stratosphere), charcoal (from global forest fires throwing ash into the stratosphere) and grains of shocked quartz.

Many old impact sites in Australia (Lake Acraman and Gosse's Bluff among them) have shocked and broken rock

million years ago
500
480
460
440
420
400
380
360
340
320
300
280
260
240
220
200
180
160
140
120
100
80
60
40
20
present

beneath them, although the crater walls, crater debris, ejected debris and meteorite fragments have long since been weathered and eroded and are now no longer visible, seriously hindering identification of old meteorite impact sites. Hence, our inability to link some mass extinctions, both major and minor, to a meteorite hit may simply be due to the difficulty we have in recognising an impact site that is deeply eroded or covered by other rocks.

Although there is strong evidence for large meteorite impacts driving mass extinction followed by rapid evolution, the jury is still out on other global geological effects of extraterrestrial hits. Nevertheless, one meteorite reaching Earth can ruin your whole day – and make your species extinct.

Sediment from inland rivers

After the deposition of the coal-bearing sequences at Mount Mulligan, about 200 million years ago, the climate changed from an icehouse to a greenhouse. As with most other greenhouse events preserved in the geological record, the reason for this climate change is unknown. What we do know is that the Australian landmass continued to rotate in an anti-clockwise direction and drifted northwards.

Twenty-five million years later, Australia had become a tropical paradise. Plant species that now thrive in far north Queensland were widespread in southern Australia, and high rainfall created numerous large inland rivers, lakes and swamps. These rivers cut through Australia, changed course and deposited

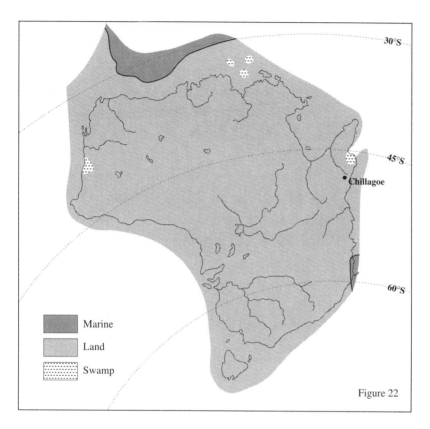

The Australian continent 180 million years ago

sands. The existence over a long period of rivers that meandered and constantly changing course left layers of sediment over the continent.

As a result, Australia was blanketed by river sands which formed the basement to the Great Artesian Basin. These sands contained very well-rounded spherical quartz grains typical of river systems, which have reworked grains many times and carried them great distances. Where there were no rivers, muds and clays were deposited in swampy billabongs.

The weight of overlying sediments hardened the river sands into a very porous sandstone which is now the host for artesian water, oil and gas in Queensland, the Northern Territory and South Australia. The oil and gas derive from the decomposition of animal material in older sediments deeper in the Great Artesian Basin. Pressure and heat convert the animal remains into oil and gas, which then migrate from the source rocks into trap rocks. The trap rocks have space between their grains, ideal for storing substances, and are capped by an impervious rock.

Artesian water derives from high rainfall periods in eastern Queensland. The last few million years of Earth history have seen five greenhouse events alternate with five icehouse events. During greenhouse events, the high rainfall in eastern Queensland has resulted in a flow of underground water down the porous permeable sands into the centre of the Great Artesian Basin. Water there has been heated and pressurised. So artesian water is stored fossil water, which is the remnant of a previous greenhouse period.

The meandering rivers left a veil of quartz sands over the Chillagoe area. Rivers in flood left minor gravels and deposited some clays, now the Gilbert River Formation, on the floor of inland lakes, swamps and bogs – the lakes were fed by large, northerly flowing, inland rivers. The mineral deposits in the Chillagoe district would have been covered by the sedimentary rocks formed from these sands, as part of the Great Artesian Basin. The cover would have protected the orebodies from weathering and erosion during an elongated period of tropical conditions.

At this time, Southern Australia was joined to Antarctica. Australia had also changed from rotating anti-clockwise and drifting northwards to rotating clockwise and drifting southwards. Between 160 and 130 million years ago, Australia and Antarctica started to stretch apart. The crust between the two thinned from 40 kilometres thick to 10 kilometres thick, and a 400-kilometre-wide rift opened up between them. Sand and silt poured into the rift from the now-elevated Antarctic and Australian continental masses. Even though Australia was still joined to Antarctica and was at the South Pole, its rivers were meandering and sand-laden; warm, high-rainfall conditions reigned; and conifers, cycads and ferns thrived.

The inland sea

Meanwhile, 140 million years ago, India started to drift away from Western Australia. And as soon as there was increased continental drift, there was also a major greenhouse event and a rise in sea level. In fact, the 400-million-year greenhouse/icehouse cycle is controlled by the drifting apart and stitching together of continents. On a grand scale, the circulation of ocean waters controls climate, and on a smaller scale, mountains influence climate; so movement of continents – which involves changes to ocean current *and* uplift of mountains – plays an important role in greenhouse/icehouse cycles.

The greenhouse climate had a profound impact on sea level, which rose – in part because the melting of polar ice caps added to the volume of water in the seas, and in part because of the expansion of heated sea water. As a result, Australia was

500 $\dfrac{\text{million}}{\text{years ago}}$
480
460
440
420
400
380
360
340
320
300
280
260
240
220
200
180
160
140
120
100
80
60
40
20
present

inundated by a warm, shallow inland sea which filled the rift between Australia and Antarctica.

Maximum sea level was reached 110 million years ago, when the continent of Australia was reduced to only four small islands. This was the last time Australia was covered by an inland sea. The early explorers, searching for the inland sea, had the right idea but they were 110 million years too late! (During this time, much of Europe was also covered by warm shallow seas, in which a great diversity of life thrived. The sea floor became covered with muds containing an abundance of limey shell fossils and much of this material can be seen today in the Mediterranean, Alpine and chalk areas of Europe.)

As the warm, shallow sea that covered Australia slowly retreated, it left a blanket of marine clay across the continent. At Chillagoe, this claystone is called the Wallumbilla Formation. Elsewhere in Australia, the clay forms the opal dirt at Coober Pedy in South Australia, and at White Cliffs and Lightning Ridge in New South Wales. The claystones commonly contain shallow-water shell fossils which, at Coober Pedy and White Cliffs, have been opalised. Dinosaur skeletons in the 110-million-year-old claystones from White Cliffs show that dinosaurs ventured into the shallow water, became trapped, died and were later fossilised. Dinosaur fossils, principally plesiosaurs, became opalised during later periods of intense weathering and silica movement. In the rocks formed at this time at Winton in central Queensland, tidal flats have preserved the footprints of more than four thousand dinosaurs. The footprints show that large dinosaurs frightened a chicken-sized bird-like dinosaur. Life was abundant in warm, wet Australia 110 million years ago.

Further evidence that Australia was at the South Pole at that time are the extraordinarily large eyes of the dinosaur fossils found in rock sequences of southern Victoria , suggesting that the dinosaurs needed better night vision than do animals today. This would have been an evolutionary adaptation to the dark conditions of the polar areas, which have long periods of winter darkness. The rocks in which the dinosaurs are found are composed of fragments of volcanic ash which have been reworked during torrential rainfall. Clearly, Antarctica was blessed with explosive volcanoes then, as it is now (Mount Erebus is one example).

The evidence for Australia having been close to the South Pole is supported by the presence of huge rocks, known as ice-rafted boulders, in the Great Artesian Basin.

Some parts of the basin contain fine-grained, white marine clays in which there are shallow marine fossils and the occasional dinosaur fossil, suggesting deposition of sediment in a bay or estuary in quiet water conditions. The clay-rich sediments also contain an occasional ice-rafted boulder that is so large that all the clay would have been removed if it had been washed by water. When glacier ice grinds over a surface, it picks up boulders. When the glacier reaches the sea, the end of it is dropped into the sea as a flotilla of icebergs. The icebergs melt and the large, ice-rafted boulders drop onto the sea floor. The story is graphically told in the opal fields, where large rounded boulders are commonly found in light-coloured, marine claystones known as 'opal dirt'. At White Cliffs, New South Wales, for example, the ice-rafted boulders are a fossiliferous quartzite.

So, while the planet was enjoying a global greenhouse, we

500 $\frac{\text{million}}{\text{years ago}}$
480
460
440
420
400
380
360
340
320
300
280
260
240
220
200
180
160
140
120
100
80
60
40
20
present

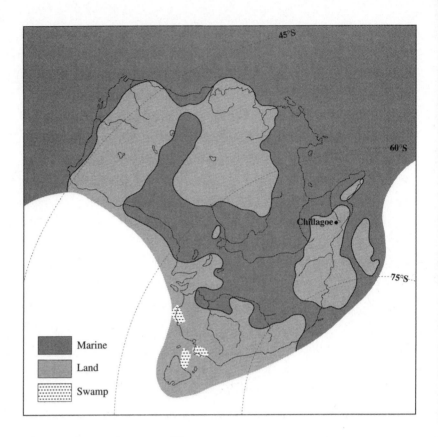

The Australian continent 120 million years ago

know that Australia was joined to Antarctica and was close to the South Pole, and that the hinterland must have been mountainous with glaciers.

Between 120 and 90 million years ago, much of the landmass of Australia was moving out of the high southern latitudes, and by 90 million years ago Australia was rotating anti-clockwise and drifting northwards.

Goodbye India

500 $\frac{\text{million}}{\text{years ago}}$
480
460
440
420
400
380
360
340
320
300
280
260
240
220
200
180
160
140
120
100
80
60
40
20
present

Meanwhile, 100 million years ago, India was drifting away from Australia at the rate of five centimetres per year. This resulted in a great stretching of the Indian Ocean. Four million years later, rifting began on the eastern coast of Australia, New Zealand started to stretch away from the east of the continent, and the Tasman Sea opened.

By 80 million years ago New Zealand had broken away from Australia and started to drift out into the Pacific Ocean, away from Australia. This eastward drift stopped only when India collided with Asia 50 million years ago. These events had a profound impact on eastern Australia, because the stresses and tensions in the rocks of Western Australia were felt right through to eastern Australia. The Chillagoe area was greatly affected by New Zealand's eastward departure.

Goodbye New Zealand, and the rise of the Great Dividing Range

In modern rifts, such as the East African Rift, the rift valley floor has subsided in a step-wise pattern. The deepest part of the rift, the medial rift, is the locus for the maximum volcanic activity. The walls of the rift valley are uplifted in a scissor-like fashion. Steep cliffs form and, out of the rift, the land slopes away from the rift valley. So, too, for ancient rifts.

As New Zealand started to drift away, the eastern edge of the Australian continent warped – in fact, there were three major events of warping as a result of the Tasman Sea opening – and the Great Dividing Range appeared. Steep scarps also formed along the eastern seaboard of Australia. In some of these areas today, the difference between the elevated plateau and the coastal plain is more than a thousand metres. Good examples are seen in the steeply incised gorge country between the New England Tableland and the north coast of New South Wales, and in far north Queensland, such as that between Kuranda and the coastal plain at Cairns.

Some rocks did not warp, instead being broken along faults. These faults had a long period of activity and every time eastern Australia was under stress from the eastward departure of New Zealand, the faults moved. At times hot water was pumped out of them. Reactivation of the faults facilitated the sporadic uplift of the Great Dividing Range.

Some of the faults were very deep and, as a result of decreasing stresses, induced a slight melting of the Earth's mantle; basalt lavas then moved up the faults. Each time Australia warped, the faults were reactivated and basalt volcanoes appeared. These volcanoes were mostly non-explosive, erupting lava that flowed down the valleys of the Great Dividing Range.

Some of the basalt that was erupted at this time carried material from deep in the mantle. Bombs of olivine-rich rocks – samples of the mantle – were ejected from the more explosive volcanoes, and other erupted material has been found to contain crystals of sapphire, zircon and diamond, which must have been brought to the surface very quickly from great depth. The weathering, erosion and concentration of the heavy gemstones from these rare explosive basalt volcanoes has produced a concentration of sapphire and diamond in eastern Australia; indeed, the sapphire fields of Queensland and New South Wales owe their origin to the opening of the Tasman Sea and the eastward drifting of New Zealand. Ironically, western New Zealand is not a basalt province and there are no gem fields in New Zealand.

The rapid rise of the Great Dividing Range changed the course of Australia's major river systems. Before the warping of eastern Australia, many major rivers flowed eastwards into the Pacific Ocean. Now, as a result of warping, these rivers had

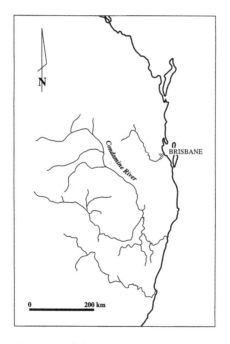

River system before the uplift of the Great Dividing range

500	million years ago
480	
460	
440	
420	
400	
380	
360	
340	
320	
300	
280	
260	
240	
220	
200	
180	
160	
140	
120	
100	
80	
60	
40	
20	
present	

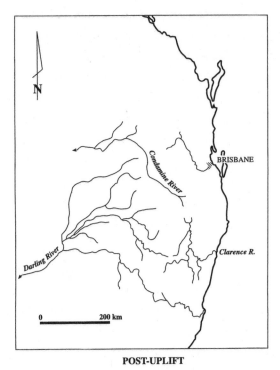

POST-UPLIFT

River piracy as a result of uplift of the Great Dividing Range

been cut in half, with some drainage eastwards into the Pacific Ocean but most westwards into the inland. For example, the easterly flowing Condamine River near Brisbane was beheaded by the rising mountain belt. The short Clarence River now flows east from the Great Dividing Range and the long Condamine River has a long inland passage before it finally reaches the ocean.

In far north Queensland, the major drainage pattern was changed with the rise of the Great Dividing Range. The rivers flowing east are short and steep, whereas those flowing inland have a long, gentle passage to the Gulf of Carpentaria. The

Great Dividing Range has a gentle slope inland and a steep slope on the coastal side, producing the spectacular gorge country along the length of eastern Australia.

Furthermore, with the rise of eastern Australia, much of the drainage water that flowed west was as underground water. It filled the pore spaces in the sands, flowing down and into the centre of the Great Artesian Basin. During the passage of the underground water from the eastern highlands, salts were dissolved in it and the water was heated. As a result, artesian water is now hot, at high pressure and saline. Australia then was warm and wet, and the Great Artesian Basin filled with water.

Today, artesian water pumped from Longreach in Queensland is two million years old. Rain that fell in eastern Queensland took that long to flow underground from coastal Queensland to Longreach. Such artesian water is fossil water and should only be used frugally, as we cannot sit around for another two million years waiting for the aquifer to recharge!

The uplift and warping of eastern Australia created stresses inland, which reactivated ancient faults. As a result, blocks of Australia moved up and down. The Flinders Ranges of South Australia, for example, were uplifted. In the tropical climate of the time the Flinders Ranges were stripped of younger sedimentary rocks and the sediment was redeposited in a large basin to the east, centred at Lake Frome. A major fault formed along the eastern edge of the Flinders Ranges, which is still active today and results in numerous earth tremors and hot springs (the Paralana Hot Springs among them). The Palmerville Fault in Queensland moved once more.

While eastern Australia was warping upwards, inland Australia was being eroded down to a plain and, in places, subsided

500 — million years ago
480 —
460 —
440 —
420 —
400 —
380 —
360 —
340 —
320 —
300 —
280 —
260 —
240 —
220 —
200 —
180 —
160 —
140 —
120 —
100 —
80 —
60 —
40 —
20 —
present

as a result of the rise of the Great Dividing Range. This is why Lake Eyre in South Australia is now below sea level. The combined effect of the retreat of the inland seas and the upwarping of the Great Dividing Range left a large continental depression in inland north Queensland called the Karumba Basin. Rivers flowing into inland Australia deposited sand, gravel and clay.

Tropical inland Australia

In inland Australia 60 million years ago, rainfall was ten times the current annual amount and the average temperature was nineteen degrees Celsius. Australia continued to stretch away from Antarctica until, 45 million years ago, it finally broke away and started to move northwards at a rapid rate. 'Rapid', that is, in terms of continental movement: the most rapid rate of drifting of continents today has been measured at 14 centimetres per year, although geological evidence suggests that in former times drifting has been as high as 18 centimetres per year.

The initial separation of Australia from Antarctica was at a rate of about twelve centimetres per year. Once Australia was well north of Antarctica, drifting slowed. Australia is currently escaping from Antarctica, moving northwards, at the rate of seven centimetres per year. In modern times, Australia has collided with Asia to form Indonesia; and this collision has resulted in frequent catastrophic earthquakes and explosive volcanoes, such as Krakatoa and Tambora, in Indonesia. A large ocean trench has formed and the ocean floor is being pushed down beneath Indonesia. Ultimately, Australia will be stitched

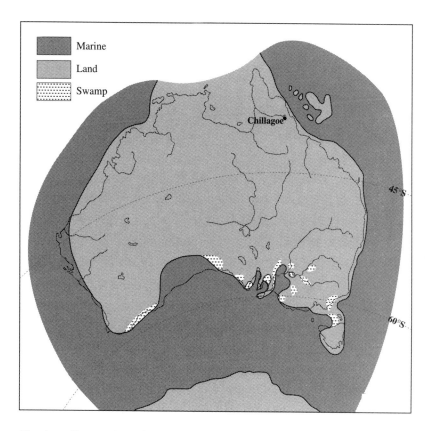

The Australian continent 65 million years ago

on to Asia. The union of these land masses will greatly change circulation in the ocean and the atmosphere, and (if the history of the last few thousand million years can be used as a guide) the planet will plunge into another icehouse.

The collision of Australia with Asia at Indonesia produces in Australia stresses that are occasionally released as very large, Richter magnitude 6 to 7, intraplate earthquakes (those within

101

a continental plate, rather than between two plates) in the unpopulated inland areas. The largest recent occurrence of such an earthquake was in 1990 in the Tennant Creek district. These intraplate earthquakes are the same type as those that occur in China where, in historical times, a single earthquake has been responsible for more than a million human casualties! If such an earthquake occurred in a highly populated area of Australia, such as a capital city or along the east coast, the effects would be similarly catastrophic. Even a 'modest' earthquake of Richter magnitude 5.4 in Newcastle, New South Wales, on 27 December 1989 left twelve people dead and hundreds injured, and a billion dollars worth of property damage.

To return to 60 million years ago, the tropical conditions in Australia persisted until about 6 million years ago, when there was a period of global cooling. This cooling led to a great change in the planet and profound evolutionary changes in the primate community, culminating in the rise of humans.

Before one jumps to conclusions that might suggest that we humans are the top of the evolutionary pile, the matter of human evolution needs to be put into perspective. Evolution and extinction are normal. Terrestrial vertebrates such as humans have an average species life of three million years. The genus *Homo* has been around for some two million years. By contrast, some organisms which we regard as primitive have been far better survivors. For example, as we have seen, bacteria have been around for a mere 3800 million years and have adapted to exist in a great diversity of environments – oxygen-rich or oxygen-poor, with or without light, at high temperatures (up to 240 degrees Celsius), at extremes of acidity or alkalinity, at high pressures or even in conditions of excessively high radiation. Bacteria are at the pinnacle of the pile of life on Earth, and it needs to be said that we humans have an ego incommensurate with our evolutionary place in Nature.

Two major factors led to the evolution of humans. The first was the comet-induced mass extinction 65 million years ago which led to the demise of the dinosaurs. The comet struck the Gulf of Mexico, ejected massive quantities of material into the atmosphere, formed huge tidal waves which went from Texas to Canada and back, destroyed the Caribbean islands with tidal waves, and blanketed the planet with dust. Dust prevented sunlight from penetrating, land and marine plants died or were stressed, and a collapse in the food chain began. The falling of ejected material onto Earth greatly heated the atmosphere and there is evidence of global forest fires at that time. Survivors lived in marine or underground terrestrial environments.

However, the planet quickly recovered. Ecological vacancies were quickly filled. The flora re-established itself, the surviving mammals thrived and diversified in the post-mass extinction tropical times because the planet was covered with lush vegetation and the dinosaurian predators had been eliminated. Again, the planet saw another period of biological experimentation and rapid evolution.

The second reason for the evolution of humans was a global cooling 6 million years ago, which forced a retreat of tropical forests into grasslands. Tree-dwelling primates evolved quickly to accommodate these changes. Some of these became extinct, but others left the trees to become our walking, ancestral primates: *Australopithicus*.

500 million years ago
480
460
440
420
400
380
360
340
320
300
280
260
240
220
200
180
160
140
120
100
80
60
40
20
present

Weathering and erosion in the warm, wet conditions 60 to 6 million years ago stripped off most of the sedimentary rocks, and the Featherbed Volcanics were exposed to the elements once again. The blanket of ash falls and ash flows around the craters of the eight volcanoes of the Featherbed Volcanics were eroded. The craters, which were once depressions, remain today as hills in what is now an inverted topography.

The exposure of Chillagoe

The weathering that stripped off the sedimentary rocks of the Great Artesian Basin exposed the mineral deposits and surrounding rocks of Chillagoe to the elements. The tropical climate produced large volumes of warm acid water which percolated down through the freshly exposed rocks, dissolving the limestone (calcium carbonate), and released huge quantities of carbon dioxide into the atmosphere. Underground, the water moved along fractures, dissolved more limestone and enlarged the caves at Chillagoe. Some of the calcium carbonate-laden water evaporated to form stalactites (hanging from the ceiling of the caves) and stalagmites (growing up from the floor). In some windy caves, the stalactites were bent or horizontal (helectites).

The limestone outcrops became pinnacles of grooved and fluted rock with the outcrop shape controlled by fractures. Much limestone was removed in solution to end up as cement in the pores of other rocks or dissolved in sea water. The removal of limestone left behind a surface composed of insoluble quartz, clay and iron oxides in the red soil so beloved of wine-makers, called terra rossa. (See colour plate 14)

Tropical weathering and magnificent minerals

The weathering of the mineral deposits at Chillagoe was responsible for the formation of a spectacular array of magnificent crystals of copper minerals. Chillagoe is well known for its world-class specimens of azurite, malachite, cuprite and native copper.

Weathering is a process that takes place at low temperatures and pressures. Water, including the oxygen and carbon dioxide dissolved in it, chemically reacts with the minerals that formed at high temperatures and pressures.

At Chillagoe, the warm rainwater reacted with the older, unstable sulphide minerals. The joints, fractures, faults and gas explosion vents were the pipelines down which large amounts of the acid rainwater could descend to attack the sulphide minerals formed over the long history of complex events. This oxidation produced massive quantities of sulphuric acid, which percolated down even deeper through the fractured rocks and vigorously corroded more minerals at Chillagoe, reacting with silicate minerals to form clay and with sulphide minerals. The areas which contain sulphides at Chillagoe – in contrast to those that have no sulphides – are very deeply weathered as a result of this deep leaching by sulphuric acid. The process is still taking place today, with the

	million years ago
500	
480	
460	
440	
420	
400	
380	
360	
340	
320	
300	
280	
260	
240	
220	
200	
180	
160	
140	
120	
100	
80	
60	
40	
20	
present	

acid, oxygen-bearing rainwater attacking sulphides, precipitating new minerals, and removing copper and other metals into the groundwaters. Once the sulphides are removed by mining, the deep weathering of sulphides and addition of metals to the groundwaters is greatly reduced.

Zoning of minerals

The Chillagoe field is best known for its secondary copper minerals formed in response to the weathering of the sulphides, which has taken place numerous times. When the geothermal systems in the area cooled and collapsed, the flow of groundwaters into the warm fractured rocks resulted in chemical reactions and the formation of new minerals. These assemblages were then overprinted by minerals formed during weathering. A mineral assemblage formed by the weathering of sulphides can also be overprinted if the land surface is uplifted, if the water table drops or if the climate changes. The history of Chillagoe is so complex that all of these events have taken place in the area. The textures of the secondary minerals showing overprinting probably represent only the most recent weathering.

Furthermore, downward oxidation of the acid water caused a crude zoning of copper minerals, which is a normal vertical zonation in any deeply weathered sulphide orebody. Close to the surface, where the most intense weathering took place, copper phosphates, arsenates and copper silicates have been preserved. Deeper down, copper carbonate azurite formed and was later altered to malachite. Below the malachite zone, cuprite formed just above the water table. This cuprite was later oxidised to tenorite and malachite.

At the water table, the weathering of the sulphide mineralisation at the Red Dome Mine produced the rare copper sulphides chalcocite and djurleite, native silver, native gold and native copper. Although there was limestone in the sequence of rocks at Chillagoe, most of the limestone at Red Dome had been replaced by silicates (for example, garnet, hedenbergite, quartz, feldspar) and sulphides (bornite, chalcopyrite). There was not enough limestone to neutralise the large quantities of sulphuric acid that percolated through the rock sequence for more than 50 million years. Furthermore, once the crack or fracture in the limestone has reacted with the acid water flowing through it, the acid waters cannot penetrate the now relatively impervious rock for further reaction.

Over time the water table has dropped, causing this zoning of minerals to be overprinted by new minerals, and causing the growth of cuprite over native copper, the oxidation of cuprite to tenorite and malachite, the pseudomorphing of azurite by malachite, the formation of brochantite and the growth of liebethenite over calcite which overgrows malachite.

Much recent material from the Red Dome Mine shows that chrysocolla and calcite have overgrown malachite, suggesting that there were times when the water table was far higher than it is at present. Rare specimens in the Australian Museum in Sydney show azurite coated by chrysocolla and fluorite, again suggesting a period of secondary mineral deposition when the water table was far higher than it is now.

The secondary minerals at Chillagoe give us an insight not only into the attack by acid groundwaters on the sulphide orebodies, but also into the great variations in the water table which Chillagoe experienced during the formation of the

million years ago
500
480
460
440
420
400
380
360
340
320
300
280
260
240
220
200
180
160
140
120
100
80
60
40
20
present

secondary minerals. Such variations are climate-induced and thus are a window onto past climatic fluctuations. However, at Chillagoe the intergrowths of secondary minerals are so complex that it is not possible to identify exactly when the overprintings took place during the last 6 million years of rapidly changing climate.

Gossan

The intensely weathered surface of an orebody is called gossan. Intense weathering near the surface at Chillagoe produced iron oxides such as limonite, goethite and haematite.

If an iron sulphide (pyrite) or iron–copper sulphide (chalcopyrite, bornite) reacts with aerated groundwater, the iron is fixed into insoluble ferric oxides such as limonite. The copper from the sulphides is also oxidised but is mobilised into the groundwaters. The sulphur from the sulphides combines with water and air to form sulphuric acid, as described previously. The copper-bearing aerated sulphuric acid attacks common silicate minerals such as feldspars to form clays. Silica is released when feldspars are destroyed and this is re-precipitated in the uppermost zones. Therefore, the uppermost part of the weathered sulphide orebody contains residual iron oxides, silica and clays. (See colour plate 15)

The weathering of carbonates has produced some interesting assemblages at Chillagoe. Because manganese and calcium are chemically similar, the small amounts of manganese substitute for calcium in the abundant calcium minerals. Manganoan carbonates have been almost totally dissolved, with porous skeletal manganese and iron oxides replaced by silica defining what was the carbonate cleavage.

Phosphate-silicate-arsenate-tungstate zone

Beneath the gossan is an iron oxide-rich zone in which the metal- and silica-bearing aerated sulphuric acid continued to descend and chemically attack minerals. This attack was savage and prolonged. After a long period of acid attack and the passing of large volumes of acid groundwaters, some of the minerals most resistant to acid attack finally broke down and released material into the groundwaters. Eventually even fossils in the limey rocks were dissolved, the calcium phosphate (apatite) in the fossils' shells broke down and phosphate entered the groundwater.

In the porous, intensely weathered iron oxide-rich rocks, the copper in the descending groundwaters combined with the breakdown products of apatite to form the dark-green water-bearing copper phosphates liebethenite and pseudomalachite. Although not yet reported from Chillagoe, the water-bearing copper phosphate turquoise is expected. (Mineral collectors should be careful because not every green copper mineral from Chillagoe is malachite; some could be a rare phosphate.)

In these iron oxide-rich rocks, the reaction between lead and phosphate in solution with clays has produced the water-bearing lead–aluminium phosphate plumbogummite (as found at Mungana). The copper and silica dissolved in the descending groundwaters combined in the iron oxide-rich rocks to form the water-bearing copper silicate chrysocolla (at

500 — million years ago
480
460
440
420
400
380
360
340
320
300
280
260
240
220
200
180
160
140
120
100
80
60
40
20
present

Red Dome, Euro Mine and Fortuna Group). Minor zinc in solution has also combined with silica in solution to form hemimorphite (for example, at Muldiva). (See colour plates 16 and 17)

Although often mis-identified or not recognised, arsenic-bearing minerals are common at Chillagoe. The weathering of the iron–arsenic sulphide (arsenopyrite) released iron (as insoluble iron oxide), soluble arsenates and sulphuric acid. In the oxide zone, the fixing of copper and arsenic from solution has occurred, with the precipitation of the water-bearing calcium–copper arsenate conichalcite (for example, at Red Dome).

Measurement of water chemistry and calculations on the stability of secondary minerals show that other copper arsenates, such as cornwallite and olivenite, are also expected at Chillagoe, although not yet recorded.

During weathering, arsenopyrite and other minerals, such as glaucodot, release cobalt into solution. This reacts with the arsenate-bearing, aerated acid groundwaters in the oxide zone to form the spectacular pink water-bearing cobalt arsenate erythrite (as seen at Red Dome).

Minor quantities of lead in the Chillagoe orebodies occur as the sulphide galena. Attack of galena by the aerated acid groundwaters produced sulphuric acid and released lead into solution. When the lead combined with arsenate, phosphate or both, then the yellowish-brown lead chloroarsenate mimetite and brown–green lead chlorophosphate pyromorphite formed (for example, at Mungana). The fact that these minerals contain chlorine shows that the groundwaters from which they formed were saline.

Probably the most unusual mineral from the highly leached iron oxide-rich rocks is 'chillagite'. For a substance to be given a mineral species name, it must occur naturally, have a unique packing of atoms and have a chemical composition between certain boundaries. Minerals are often named because of their chemistry (for example, arsenopyrite), after a famous mineralogist or collector (Professor Eugen Stumpfl, for example, has two minerals named in his honour – stumpflite and eugenite) or after the location where the mineral was first discovered (for example, brokenhillite). 'Chillagite' is, unfortunately, a discredited mineral species because it is chemically between wulfenite (lead molybdenum oxide) and stolzite (lead tungsten oxide). The correct name for 'chillagite' is tungstenian wulfenite. However, its composition is so unusual that a case could be mounted to have it classified as a new mineral, unique to the Christmas Gift Mine at Chillagoe.

The components of 'chillagite' come from a diversity of minerals which are uncommon in the orebodies in the Chillagoe district. Its tungsten derives from the weathering of the calcium tungstate scheelite, the molybdenum from the weathering of the molybdenum sulphide molybdenite, and the lead from the weathering of galena (lead sulphide).

Carbonate zone

The Chillagoe field is best known for its carbonates of copper. The carbonate zone occurs beneath the gossan and oxide-rich rocks and, although the carbonate zone is dominated by iron oxides, the brightly coloured copper carbonates are widespread.

million years ago

500
480
460
440
420
400
380
360
340
320
300
280
260
240
220
200
180
160
140
120
100
80
60
40
20

present

Colour in minerals has three possible causes. If a mineral structure is twisted or contains stray atoms (large or small), it can become coloured (for example, blue quartz, green lead-rich orthoclase, lilac lithium-bearing minerals). Colour can also be due to myriads of inclusions of solids, liquids or gas (for example, gas inclusions impart a pink colour to diamond, fluid inclusions make quartz milky, solid rutile inclusions give a smoky colour to quartz). The green and blue copper minerals, the pink and blue cobalt minerals, the green, brown and yellow iron minerals and the green, orange and violet chromium minerals are coloured because there are a group of chemical elements called the transition elements which have coloured compounds. Minerals from Chillagoe are coloured because they contain the transition elements, such as copper, iron and cobalt.

Intense leaching over long periods of time has removed much of the upper portions of the orebodies at Chillagoe. Most of the rock has been removed into the groundwaters and only the residual iron oxide minerals remain, in porous cavernous material. New carbonate minerals were deposited in these pores and cavities as a result of groundwater–mineral reactions over a long period of time. The constant growth of minerals has led to the growth of very coarse-grained carbonate minerals, and the formation of the carbonate zone.

Calcite (calcium carbonate) is a common mineral in the carbonate zone. The calcite-bearing rocks are very porous and permeable. As calcite is not only soluble in water but it is extremely reactive with acid water, every time the rocks have been bent, broken, heated, flushed with steam or hot water or weathered, calcite has been redissolved and re-precipitated.

Cavities in the porous iron oxide rocks are lined with calcite, which in turn is overprinted by azurite and malachite. The inverse is also common, and many spectacular specimens of copper carbonates, especially malachite, are dusted and coated with a thin film of calcite. This calcite appears greenish. In weathered rocks calcite is pure-white calcium carbonate, whereas calcite which has formed from hot water or steam is commonly pink manganoan calcite or orange–brown ferroan calcite.

Extremely acid aerated groundwaters formed azurite, the spectacular blue water-bearing copper carbonate. Large terminated crystals of azurite are common in the Red Dome Mine and every old mine in the Chillagoe field, especially Griffiths Claim, Eclipse Mine (Muldiva), Magazine Face and Ruddygore. During intense weathering, azurite precipitates well above the water table when copper-bearing acid groundwaters chemically react with carbon dioxide both in the groundwater and released from acid-attacking limestone. Azurite is very common from the secondary zone of many mineral deposits in Australia: this is a reflection of the long history of tropical weathering that Australia has enjoyed over the last 100 million years. (See colour plates 19, 20, 21, 22 and 23)

In contrast to the green water-bearing malachite, azurite forms in more acid groundwater conditions. If the azurite and very acid groundwater were near limestone, the groundwater would have continued to react with the limestones. Limestone is able to reduce the acidity of the groundwaters, thus releasing more carbon dioxide into the atmosphere. When azurite reacts with groundwater, the reaction derives carbon dioxide from the

million
500 years ago
480
460
440
420
400
380
360
340
320
300
280
260
240
220
200
180
160
140
120
100
80
60
40
20
present

groundwater and copper from the pre-existing azurite. In this way, azurite is pseudomorphed by malachite ($2Cu_2CO_3(OH)_2$ (azurite) + CO_2 = $2Cu_2(CO_3)_2(OH)_2$ (malachite) + H_2O).

The pseudomorphing of azurite by malachite at Chillagoe shows that there has been a long history of descending copper-bearing acid groundwaters, which first reacted with limestone to produce azurite and, when the copper in solution was spent, continued to react with the limestones. The pitted nature of many of the crystal faces of the azurite and malachite show that when the water table dropped, these minerals were partially redissolved in acid waters and the copper was moved in solution ($Cu_2(CO_3)_2(OH)_2$ (malachite) + $3H^+$ (acid) = $2Cu^{2+}$ + HCO^{3-} + $2H_2O$).

The release of copper in solution allows the formation of other copper minerals typical of long periods of intense weathering. The copper phosphates, copper arsenates and copper silicates, or the reformation of azurite at depth, result from just such fixing of the copper released into solution during long intense weathering. The small amounts of brochantite (water-bearing copper sulphate) formed as a result of the release of copper into groundwater from the breakdown of earlier malachite induced by the dropping of the water table (for example, at Red Dome Mine and McIlraith Mine).

The growth of rare native silver on the surface of malachite crystals again suggests that the water table has dropped – because malachite is typical of the upper zone of weathering, whereas native silver is typical of the lowermost weathering zone.

The lead carbonate cerussite is common in many of the mines in the Chillagoe district (Red Dome, Muldiva and Eclipse Mine among them). Twinned white lustrous crystals of cerussite which have grown on azurite show that the lead in groundwaters combined with carbon dioxide that had been released from the attack of acid waters on limestone. Most cerussite was collected late last century (for example, at Eclipse Mine) and is now in museum collections. However, at Red Dome pore spaces in spongy iron oxide rocks filled by cerussite are widespread.

The zinc sulphide sphalerite at Chillagoe was dissolved by the acid, oxygenated groundwaters. Sulphuric acid formed and zinc was removed in solution in groundwaters. Although smithsonite is a very common zinc carbonate in nature, it is rare at Chillagoe because of the extreme acidity of the ground-waters. Under these conditions, zinc carbonate is soluble and normally does not precipitate in the weathered rocks above the orebodies. However, rare botryoidal smithsonite has been col-lected at some localities.

The green-to-blue, water-bearing copper–zinc carbonates aurichalcite and rosasite are also rare. Again, this is because of the long exposure of the Chillagoe orebodies to large volumes of acid groundwater. It is only in areas dominated by limestone that such minerals are stable. For example, fluffy balls of rosa-site growing on marble from Red Dome have been collected, as have aurichalcite-filled fractures in limestone from the Penzance Mine.

500 million years ago
480
460
440
420
400
380
360
340
320
300
280
260
240
220
200
180
160
140
120
100
80
60
40
20
present

Sulphate zone

The intense weathering of sulphides, it has been explained, forms sulphuric acid. The sulphuric acid carries metals in solution and also combines with metals to precipitate sulphate minerals. Most sulphate minerals are slightly soluble and will not be preserved if weathering has been intense or long-lived. However, lead sulphate, like any other lead mineral, is very insoluble.

Anglesite, the lead sulphate, occurs beneath the carbonate zone at Chillagoe and commonly has grown on top of copper carbonates as a result of the rise of the water table. The anglesite crystals occur as stellate masses lining cavities in iron oxides, in copper carbonates and overprinting cerussite (for example, at Christmas Gift Mine). The presence of anglesite as the only sulphate from the Chillagoe field again confirms that the area has enjoyed a long history of intense weathering. (Plate 22)

Supergene enrichment zone

The supergene zone at Chillagoe is characterised by spectacular crystals and masses of the copper oxide cuprite. Cavities in massive cuprite lined with large terminated crystals of cuprite were prized by collectors, as were intergrowths of cuprite with native copper. These cavities were old caves in limestone which were later filled by native copper and cuprite. One such cavity in the high wall of the Red Dome pit has been the latest source of most of the spectacular ruby-red cuprite crystals and native copper. Massive cuprite is common and cuprite crystals are normally present in cavities in the massive cuprite.

The intergrowths of native copper and cuprite show that the water table has dropped from where oxides are stable to where native copper was once stable. Other specimens show that either the water table dropped greatly or the groundwater was channelled away in faults because cuprite has reacted to the more oxidised copper oxide tenorite, which in turn has reacted to the copper mineral malachite. The tenorite does not occur as crystals. The assemblage has been veined by pseudomalachite, a mineral which forms in the upper zones or by extreme oxidation, again suggesting re-oxidation and prolonged intense weathering.

A fibrous orange mineral known as 'chalcotrichtite' is a variety of cuprite, not a distinct mineral species. Isolated crystals and stellate masses have been observed. However, unlike cuprite (which occurs at the base of the weathered profile), 'chalcotrichtite' occurs high in the weathered profile in iron oxide-rich rocks (for example, at Christmas Gift Mine). Normally it can be seen only under a hand lens or a microscope. (See colour plates 24, 25, 26, 27, 28 and 29)

Native copper has formed at the water table in the Chillagoe area, most commonly occurring as wire. Hairy native copper coated with black tenorite and large massive plates of native copper have been recovered from the current mining operations at Red Dome. Other deposits (for example, at Muldiva, Dorothy Mine, Ruddygore) are also well-known for native copper specimens. A few, very rare specimens of wire malachite have been recovered from the Red Dome Mine. Other wire malachite specimens are overgrown with calcite on a malachite basement. These specimens show that the formation of wire

million years ago

500
480
460
440
420
400
380
360
340
320
300
280
260
240
220
200
180
160
140
120
100
80
60
40
20
present

native copper at the old water table was followed by a drop in the water table. The native copper then reacted with acid, aerated, carbon dioxide-bearing water and was pseudomorphed to form malachite.

Native copper, and to a lesser extent native silver and native gold, have been precipitated in fractures in marble at the water table. In this setting, the marble acted as a buffer for descending acid groundwaters which were not able to attack and redissolve the native copper. Some of the most spectacular specimens of native copper from Red Dome grow on glassy calcite crystals.

Beneath the native copper, supergene copper sulphides occur in a narrow, high-grade irregular zone. This zone is characterised by the absence of the sooty to deep-blue covellite and contains both supergene chalcocite and djurleite. These copper-rich minerals are usually massive and have contributed greatly to the copper content of the run of mine ore.

The Chillagoe caves

Caves form for a diversity of reasons. Many basalt lavas contain caves that were the original pipelines for the subsurface flowing of molten rock (for example, the Undara lava tubes). Other rocks become cavernous because salt spray soaks into the pores of the rock, the salt crystallises and the forces of crystallisation break out small quantities of the host rock. The honeycomb weathering, so typical of sandstones in coastal areas, is the first stage of the cave-formation process.

Caves in limestone are common. This is because the main mineral in limestone (calcite or calcium carbonate) is slightly soluble in water. Furthermore, calcite is more soluble in cold water than in hot water. Rainwater is acid, and the chemical reaction of acid on carbonate dissolves the limestone. Hence, no matter whether Chillagoe enjoyed an icehouse (with cold groundwaters) or a greenhouse (with large volumes of acid groundwaters), the limestone dissolved to form caves.

We do not know for certain when the process of cave formation from limestone solution at Chillagoe began, but there is some evidence that it began 300 million years ago, at the time of hot spring activity. What we do know is that the continent of Australia enjoyed warm, wet, tropical conditions between 60 and 35 million years ago and again between 24 and 6 million years ago. At these times, very large volumes of warm acid rainwater would have percolated down cracks, fractures and joints and dissolved the Chillagoe limestone.

Although much limestone has been removed in solution, the dry tropical climate at Chillagoe has allowed the partial redeposition of limestone as stalactites and stalagmites. Helectites have been recorded in some of the windy caves. In many caves, the formations contain a small admixture of extremely fine-grained iron oxide which imparts orange and red colours to them. Spectacular tree roots project deep into the caves in search of water, nutrients being one attraction, and the underground springs and watercourses being other attractions.

There is abundant evidence that the caves were used by Australia's original inhabitants before they were discovered by European prospectors in 1874. In the Walkunder Arch Cave,

500 million years ago
480
460
440
420
400
380
360
340
320
300
280
260
240
220
200
180
160
140
120
100
80
60
40
20
present

the numerous generations of Aboriginal cave paintings have been dated by a technique known as accelerator mass spectrometry. Minute samples of desert varnish, a fine-coating carbon-bearing material which forms over surfaces, showed that at least three layers of previous paintings underlaying the present ones were more than 25,000 years old. Measured ages were from 29,700 years to 3340 years. The ages of the cave paintings at Chillagoe show that Australian aboriginal rock art is probably as old as, or even older than, the well-publicised numerous palaeolithic cave art paintings in France and Spain.

In 1891, the caves had been photographed by the Muldiva photographer Henry Livesey and, in a decision of great foresight, the Queensland Minister for Mines attempted to have as many caves as possible excised from mining leases. The preservation of the caves since the earliest mining activity, the promotion of scientific research on the caves by various mine managers, research by the Royal Geographical Society of Queensland and an interest in the caves by local identities are such that the pristine caves are now part of a National Park. This is in stark contrast with the former and present policy of the State Department of Mines: not to collect valuable mineral specimens for museums!

The caves are unique ecologies for a diversity of bats (specifically, bent-wing bats *Miniopterus schreibersii*, *Miniopterus australis*; western cave bat *Vespadelus caurinus*; sheath-tailed bat *Taphozous georgianus*; eastern horseshoe bat *Rhinolophus megaphyllus*; diadem leaf-nosed bat *Hipposideros diadema*) and birds (grey swiftlet *Collocalia francica*). Both the bats and birds fly in darkness in the caves by using sonar navigation.

Global cooling and Chillagoe

With the beginning of the global cooling 6 million years ago, conditions at Chillagoe changed greatly. In these times, the Chillagoe caves were the home for fauna trying to escape the changing global climatic conditions. Although Australia was in the tropics, the global cooling affected the Australian landmass: glaciers covered alpine southern Australia, and inland Australia had a cool, dry, windy climate; the major sand dunes of inland Australia formed during these glacial times (only to be vegetated and stabilised during interglacial times); the sea level was lower and continental Australia was connected to Tasmania and Papua New Guinea by land bridges. Furthermore, the strong dry winds carried sea spray well inland, where the salt began to concentrate in inland depressions, lakes and evaporative areas. (The salt that causes the current salinity problems in much of Australia is this salt that was blown inland during the recent glaciation.)

The resultant retreat of the wet tropical rainforest in the Chillagoe area is still evident today. During the last 2.4 million years, there have been five icehouse events separated by greenhouse events. (It is not known whether the next major climate change will be to another icehouse or another greenhouse.) The climate at Chillagoe changed from wet tropical conditions to arid conditions, with significant changes to the flora and fauna happening as a result. The same changes occurred elsewhere in the world during these icehouses; for example, the forests of the Amazon Basin were reduced to ten per cent of their present area.

million
500 ───────
years ago
480 ───
460 ───
440 ───
420 ───
400 ───
380 ───
360 ───
340 ───
320 ───
300 ───
280 ───
260 ───
240 ───
220 ───
200 ───
180 ───
160 ───
140 ───
120 ───
100 ───
80 ───
60 ───
40 ───
20 ───
present

The most recent ice sheets started to retreat 14,000 years ago, and the sea level started to rise. The last ice age ended 8000 years ago, when the climate at Chillagoe changed from arid to the present-day dry tropical conditions. The rainforest of the last greenhouse, which had survived the arid times, changed to today's dry tropical vegetation, composed of open woodlands of ironwood and bloodwood. Refugees from previous greenhouse times adapted from the wet tropical conditions to dry tropical conditions. These refugees are still present on all the limestone outcrops in the Chillagoe district because the limestone stores water in fractures, pores and caves. Examples of limestone-hosted rainforest refugees are the fig trees, kurrajong trees, helicopter trees, batswing coral trees and strychnine bushes. All over Australia, kurrajong trees thrive on calcium-rich alkaline soils which are most commonly developed on limestone. The fig trees at Chillagoe have adapted from wet tropical to dry tropical conditions by becoming deciduous.

Chillagoe faults and water: the present situation

Both the cave formation and the sulphide mineral weathering are processes that have taken place sporadically over hundreds of millions of years and continue today in response to the current dry tropical climate. The cave system at Chillagoe is still active, with warm acid rainwater dissolving and re-precipitating the limestone. Weathering of sulphides is currently taking place with warm acid aerated waters mobilising metals, producing secondary minerals and forming sulphuric acid.

The evidence for this has been provided by measurements

and sampling taken in deep diamond drill holes at Mungana, which show that the groundwater above the unexploited Mungana base metal-gold deposit is acid, aerated and at a temperature of more than thirty degrees Celsius. Furthermore, the water is saturated with metals and is in equilibrium with the secondary copper–arsenic and lead–tungsten–molybdenum minerals at depth. This shows that the unexposed Mungana orebody is currently undergoing weathering of the secondary copper arsenate and lead tungstate–molybdate minerals which formed over a long history of intense weathering. And weathering is currently shedding the metals and sulphuric acid into the groundwater. The only way to stop this natural process of pollution is to remove the oxidised orebody by mining! The weathering of orebodies and resultant extensive natural pollution can be traced in soil, river sediment and groundwater by using techniques that have been used for decades to locate mineral deposits.

Very deep oxidation has taken place in north–south faults in the Red Dome pit. The age of the faults is not known but they clearly have been the conduit for descending acid waters for a long period of time. Water has moved down the broken rocks in the fault zone and, because weathering is a process which involves the expansion of rocks, the fault zones have been further broken. Over time, warm fluids have moved up fault zones and cool fluids have descended faults. In all cases, the fluids have reacted with the enclosing rocks. The fault zones are characterised by the presence of limonite, apple-green-coloured copper-bearing nontronite and minor cavities. Extremely fine-grained fibres of cuprite (chalcotrichtite variety) and hairy

million
500 years ago
480
460
440
420
400
380
360
340
320
300
280
260
240
220
200
180
160
140
120
100
80
60
40
20
present

native copper coat limonite line cavities. The cavities are rarely lined with calcite displaying the dog-tooth spar shape; the calcite is well-crystallised and glassy, and contains very rare inclusions of native copper. In places, the calcite is covered with very fine-grained hairy native copper.

The coatings of cuprite and native copper formed during weathering, whereas the inclusions of native copper within the calcite formed from hot fluids, probably from the last pulses of metal-laden steam moving up faults upon cooling of the Featherbed volcanic event 280 million years ago. It would be expected that copper sulphides would have formed from this metal-laden steam, but the presence of native copper shows that the last event of steam contained no sulphur, although it is common in most steam vents, geysers and hot springs.

In the Red Dome Mine area, the natural drainage is to the north-west, with recharge in the south-east. In the current mining operations, groundwater movement is stopped by a series of impervious clay-filled north–south faults. The main fault zone, which dips at seventy to eighty degrees to the north-west, is also filled with impervious swollen clays, the groundwater is dammed on the eastern side of this fault and the groundwater is an immobile perched aquifer. This modern groundwater flow shows that oxidised acid mine waters are not draining into the cave systems and, if the perched aquifer broke, mine waters would drain away from the caves.

Clearly, the ancient history of the Chillagoe area is still in the making. Rare minor earth tremors occur as a result of stresses which reactivate faults and release energy as earth tremors. To the south of Chillagoe in an extensive volcanic field, in the Undara to Mount Surprise area although the last volcanic eruptions were 17,000 years ago. Weathering and erosion are still taking place and, in response, the land is rising and being stripped of new soils. (See colour plate 30)

The ancient history of Chillagoe shows that the planet is still dynamic. Rocks are compressed, stretched, bent and broken with great regularity. Masses of molten rock move and explode at the surface, and these new hot rocks are cooled by groundwaters. The land surface is continually rising and falling and being reshaped by the elements. Climate has always changed, and continues to fluctuate between greenhouse and icehouse. It is these constant changes to the Earth's crust, the oceans and the atmosphere that drive the continual changes to life on Earth.

million
500 years ago
480
460
440
420
400
380
360
340
320
300
280
260
240
220
200
180
160
140
120
100
80
60
40
20

present

Part Two

THE RECENT HISTORY OF CHILLAGOE

For some time the whole of the Cairns hinterland has been a significant producer of tin (at Irvinebank, Herberton, Mount Garnet, Ravenshoe, for example), tungsten, molybdenum and bismuth (Wolfram Camp, Mount Carbine), gold (Palmer River, Georgetown, Forsayth) and base metals (for example, Herberton, Chillagoe). This part of the book looks at the last century of exploration, mining and smelting at Chillagoe.

Despite reputations and fortunes having been made and lost on mining scandals, and despite political intrigue and a long history of mining, there has been only one profitable mine in the Chillagoe field. It is the current operation, the Red Dome gold and copper mine, and it has been profitable only since it was acquired by Niugini Mining Ltd in 1991. However, at the turn of the century, the name Chillagoe was as well known in mining and stock exchange circles as Broken Hill, Mount Lyell, Kalgoorlie and Mount Morgan.

The first era

Far north Queensland, like the rest of Australia, was first settled by pastoralists, prospectors and miners, who took great risks with their lives and investments. In pastoral development, John Atherton was perhaps best known, while the development of mining in the Cairns hinterland can be directly credited to John Moffat, who arrived in Australia in 1862. Moffat was one of the few discoverers and developers of mines in Australia who actually personally reaped the financial benefits of his initiatives.

During the 1860s, the world-class mining fields of Mount Lyell (copper and gold), Mount Bischoff (tin), Broken Hill (silver, lead and zinc), Cobar (copper and gold), Kalgoorlie (gold), Mount Morgan (copper and gold) and Mount Isa (silver, lead and zinc) had not been discovered. Copper mining in South Australia (at Moonta, Kadina and Wallaroo), gold mining in New South Wales and Victoria, and coal mining in New South Wales were the only significant mining operations in Australia. At that time, the world markets acquired tin and copper from the mines of Cornwall (England) and the Erzgebirge (Saxony). By Moffat's death in 1918, Queensland had produced 30 million pounds worth of tin and copper.

The Moffat empire began modestly with the development of numerous mining and smelting operations in the Herberton tin fields. With the discovery of fabulous gold deposits in New South Wales and Victoria in the 1850s, the anti-clockwise exploration of the Australian continent for gold began. An 1874 expedition down the Walsh River in search of mineral deposits by James Venture Mulligan (the discoverer of the Palmer Goldfield) noticed that the local Aborigines retreated in fear into caves. As the majority of caves in the area occur in the Chillagoe limestone, Mulligan must have been the first explorer in the Chillagoe district, but it appears that he did not discover copper minerals on this particular expedition. It is not known who named the district Chillagoe – a name that derives from an old sea shanty.

In 1883, Mulligan and John Hammond were employed by Moffat and associates on an unpublicised expedition in search of copper down the eastern side of the Walsh River. Mulligan recorded showings of copper minerals which occur at the surface as the distinctive green malachite and blue azurite. A prospecting expedition in the mid-1880s down the Walsh by Charles O Garbutt and Samuel Delaney was also made in search of copper. At that time the copper market was booming, with copper metal fetching more than eighty pounds per ton.

Because of the westward spread of mining camps and their need for beef, William Atherton from Emerald End near Mareeba explored the Walsh River in 1887 for pastoral country. In June–July 1887, John Moffat sent a prospecting party, consisting of Anthony Linedale and Peter Moffat, to follow up the findings by the 1883 Mulligan–Hammond expedition. Linedale and Moffat were successful, finding azurite and native copper at surface, and they pegged many outcrops of secondary copper minerals. Other independent prospectors (the Byrnes brothers, John James) also discovered copper mineralisation in outcrop (Boomerang Mine), in what was to become the Calcifer field. The Byrnes brothers and James became embroiled in litigation over the claims at Calcifer, as John Moffat and his associates had applied for twenty claims varying in area from five to forty acres; they had named the claims after Gilbert and Sullivan or Shakespearian characters.

On 20 April 1888, Atherton applied for seven pastoral leases (Chillagoe numbers 1 to 7). He intended to stay, building a substantial timber homestead on the banks of Chillagoe Creek. The Byrnes brothers returned to their trade – butchery – in order to service the anticipated increase in population at Chillagoe.

In October 1888, John Moffat and Anthony Linedale visited all the leases in the Chillagoe field as well as the caves. On the return journey, Moffat visited his leases in the Featherbed

Range in an area which later became the Koorboora tin field. Because competitors had pegged only eight claims, Moffat was able to monopolise the field. He brought machinery and supplies overland on horse-drawn wagons from Port Douglas, north of Cairns.

Moffat sought expert advice on the mining potential of the Chillagoe field. His choice was a mining engineer, Dr James Robertson of Newcastle, New South Wales, the man who in 1882 had dismissed the Mount Morgan field as worthless (although it was in fact a very rich deposit) and had written favourably on two worthless tin leases near Irvinebank owned by Moffat! Robertson was true to form and advised Moffat that in the Chillagoe field the deposits were fissure lodes which went to great depths and would provide great profits.

The consequent development of the Chillagoe field was important in opening up vast tracts of far north Queensland, but expected dividends did not flow to shareholders in the mining companies. Like many mining fields, there were rich surface outcrops of secondary mineralisation naturally enriched slowly by a long history of weathering, but its potential was exaggerated by entrepreneurs seeking rapid personal enrichment. The change in metal content and type of ore mineral with depth at Chillagoe led to mining and treatment difficulties.

Nevertheless, in the early history of the field, hopes were high that fortunes could be made and there was litigation involving leases, boundary disputes and the sale of prospective and worthless leases at inflated prices by speculators. However, because Moffat owned most of the leases, trading in leases and wild speculation was far less rife than at other fields.

Lease consolidation led to the holding of the Wandoo and Delaney Diggings by Delaney, Garbutt and Mulligan. However, Moffat's early entry into the field with prospecting leases, later converted to mining leases, was such that Moffat essentially owned the field comprising the Atherton, Boomerang, Cyclone, Desdemona, Dorothy, Fortunata, Girofla, Griffith, Hensey, Hobson, Magazine Face, Martha, McIlraith, McTavish, Miles, Mollie, Nellie, O'Hara, Penzance, Pinafore, Portia, Queensland, Ruddygore, Silver North and Tea Tree leases. (See colour plates 31 and 32)

In 1889, John Moffat used James Robertson's report to promote the Chillagoe field which, for all practical purposes, he owned. Mining investors from South Australia, Victoria and New South Wales were unsuccessfully encouraged to provide capital. Then the 1890–91 depression dried up risk capital and Moffat concentrated his efforts in lease acquisition, at Irvinebank, of the fabulously rich pipe deposit of tin, the Vulcan Mine.

In the early 1890s, the depression, isolation, drought, bushfires and hardships on the field drove away the few remaining prospectors who had set up camp near Atherton's homestead on Chillagoe Creek. During these difficult times, John Moffat continued to purchase leases and spent 30,000 pounds in building smelters at his Calcifer (1894) and Girofla Mines (1896). Slag piles still remain at these mines as a reminder of these times. Moffat had 'bought straw hats in winter' and was poised to profit from the inevitable next mining boom.

Calcifer

The Calcifer field derives from the original name Calcufer, composed of Latin abbreviations for limestone (calx), copper (cuprum) and iron (ferrum). John Moffat erected smelters here in July 1884. These were the first smelters in the Chillagoe field and consisted of a crusher, jigs, fan-blasted iron cupolas and two steam engines to drive it all. The machinery cost 2000 pounds and was bought from the old silver mines at Newell-town (in the Herberton field) and reassembled near a spring at Calcifer.

Ore from the Calcifer field was selectively mined, hand-picked and smelted on site. The mines and smelter supported a town with homes, hotels, banks, a school and a hospital. During the first thirty months of operations, 4183 tons of ore were smelted for a return of 831 tons of copper matte valued at 29,795 pounds. Calcifer, like so many other mining camps, was touted by the promoters and sharks as the new Broken Hill – so much so that there was a speculative land boom in the town of Calcifer in 1900! However, the smelters closed in 1903, and by 1907 the bright new hope was a ghost town.

The Calcifer smelters were very inefficient and the slag was retreated in 1912. Over the years small operators took parcels of ore from the Boomerang, Harpers and Christmas Gift Mines in the Calcifer field for smelting at the centralised Chillagoe smelters, but ore reserves did not allow Calcifer to develop into a second Broken Hill. Furthermore, Calcifer was so isolated that the biggest single cost was transport, which made the mining operations marginal. In many ways, the economic prosperity of the Calcifer operations were tied to the economic prosperity of Chillagoe; and if Chillagoe coughed, Calcifer died.

The second era

John Moffat did not have to wait long for the second era at Chillagoe. Capital was attracted as a result of a visit in 1896 to the field by Melbourne and Adelaide mining and smelting entrepreneurs. With the success of Broken Hill in the late 1880s and early 1890s resulting in astonishingly high dividends, and with the development of new technology and the industrialisation of Australia, risk capital was available to repeat such good investments.

Modern, profitable state-of-the-art smelters and refineries had been built at Port Pirie in South Australia. There was a great spirit of optimism in the Australian mining industry, with the recent successes of Mount Lyell, Mount Bischoff, Bendigo, Kalgoorlie and Broken Hill, so capital was raised for the development of the Chillagoe field. Development included the building of smelters and a railway – the camps in the Chillagoe field had previously been serviced by bush tracks, which made the provisioning of stores and the transport of ore prohibitive. A railway would open up the whole province.

Muldiva – the new Broken Hill?

Hard times had reached John Moffat, who in the 1890s relinquished a number of the leases in the Chillagoe field and kept only those that he considered the most prospective. He concentrated on his silver-rich leases at Muldiva, twenty-five kilometres south-east of Chillagoe. The high price of silver and the fabulous riches from the Broken Hill silver mines in the 1880s had led to the optimistic establishment of Muldiva after discovery of silver there in 1888 by John Moffat's prospecting party. Samuel Delaney had registered the leases on 15 August 1889 on behalf of Moffat, and stockbroking interests were keen to set up a company quickly to capitalise on the high silver price and the euphoria of Broken Hill. The Muldiva Silver Mining and Smelting Company was incorporated on 21 November 1890 and successfully floated on the stock exchange.

The vendors of the Muldiva Silver Mining and Smelting Company unloaded their shares onto the bullish market. Great profits were made by mining the speculative market before the first ton of ore was mined. Capital raised on the market was used to purchase a crusher, smelters comprising two reverberatory furnaces with fans for blasting air into the furnaces, and two thirty-horsepower engines to drive the plant. Long water races and a dam were constructed. Because of the lack of coal or other energy sources near the isolated Muldiva camp, charcoal burners were established. Smelting a mixture of silver oxide and sulphide ore with a flux and charcoal is a silver smelting technique known since the Middle Ages.

The company blew in the smelter in January 1892, with a monthly production of 4000 to 5000 ounces of silver. Production was far less than planned because of machinery failures and difficulties in smelting the mineralogically complex ore. A town that boasted a branch of the Bank of North Queensland was established to service the operation which, in its short life, produced 235,000 ounces of silver bullion. The company never paid a dividend.

Muldiva was so remote that its bullion often reached the market months after smelting. Its operations, too, were very sensitive to metal price fluctuations. With the depression of the 1890s and the collapse in the silver price, the smelters closed on 21 May 1893. The machinery and smelter were transported to Moffat's operations at Girofla in 1896 and Muldiva became a ghost town.

Girofla

The mines along Opera Creek (Dorothy, Girofla, Griffiths Hill, Lady Jane, Magazine Face and Nordville) were all serviced by the township of Mungana. The relocated Muldiva smelters treated ore mainly from Girofla and Lady Jane, with minor ore shipments from the other deposits. Slag still remains on site from these smelting operations. The mines closed with the closure of the Chillagoe smelters in 1914. There was a limited revival in the period 1919–30, when the Queensland government acquired the interests of Fred Reid's Mungana Mines Limited. Successful exploration interest in the Chillagoe field is currently taking place along Opera Creek (Griffiths Hill, Lady Jane and Girofla) and in an extension of the field to a previously unexploited deposit (NW Mungana).

At its height, the town of Mungana boasted churches, shops, hotels, restaurants and a railway terminus. All sorts of stories exist about main-street gunfights, with the burial of the losers in the main street, but Mungana died a slow death over fifty years, and only a railway siding and paddocks overgrown with chinky bush exist now.

At Girofla, the shaft, open pit and crank of a massive beam pump remain, and at Lady Jane, the shaft stonework, beam pump and crusher foundations are preserved. In the Mungana district, some of the original stonework on the railway line is still in good condition.

To the east of Mungana was the Shannon–Zillmanton line of lode. Numerous pits exploited the secondary copper ore from Zillmanton. The spongy silica–iron sulphide ore (now known to be gold-bearing) created smelter problems, as did its high zinc sulphide content. A town of 8000 was established to service the mines, which are now flooded. Numerous dumps, stonework around shafts and pump housings, and the foundations of two mills, are all that remain. The mine sites must have once been cleared land buzzing with activity, but now the area has returned to eucalypt and spear grass.

Chillagoe Proprietary Limited

John Moffat had had great success with tin mining and smelting in the Irvinebank area and, despite the disappointment of Muldiva silver operations, he was persistently trying to establish Chillagoe as a major mining field. On 29 November 1897, an agreement between John Moffat (as vendor) with William Knox (Director of BHP and The Mount Lyell Mining and Railway Company), Malcolm McEachern (Chairman of McIlwraith-McEachern Shipping Line and the Burns Philp Company), Alfred Tolhurst (Melbourne stockbroker), Charles W Chapman

(Adelaide smelter and refinery owner) and Hermann Schlapp (world-renowned Broken Hill metallurgist) were signed to establish the Chillagoe Proprietary Limited. McEachern and Chapman had previously visited Chillagoe in 1896 as Moffat's guests, in his efforts to promote the field to the money markets.

Now that Knox and associates had secured the rights to the Chillagoe field, a change in legislation was necessary to allow the building of a railway, the construction of smelters and the granting of long-term leases. With such distinguished subscribers to Chillagoe Proprietary Limited, it was possible to have the Mareeba to Chillagoe Railway Act expedited through the Queensland parliament within a month of the agreement having been signed. The Act granted a fifty-year mining lease over 729 hectares, gave the first right of refusal after fifty years for the purchasing of the leases back to the Queensland government, gave legislative approval for the building of a private railway and dismissed the labour requirements required for the servicing of granted mining leases. This was an exceptionally generous Act of the Queensland parliament.

A mining entrepreneur, James Smith Reid, who had also visited the field in 1896 with McEachern, Chapman and Moffat, formed Chillagoe Railway and Mines Limited. Reid, a BHP director, had once been a newspaper proprietor on the Ravenswood goldfields in north Queensland. He was the driving force behind a number of mining company promotions. He tried to make the Chillagoe mining field an economic success against formidable odds, and provided employment for five thousand people, finally making enormous profits from his share sales in 1901.

Chillagoe Railway and Mines Ltd had a nominal capital of one million pounds, was registered on 16 June, 1898, and appointed Alex Stewart (from BHP in Broken Hill) as general manager. In 1898, John Moffat sold his shareholding in Chillagoe Proprietary Limited and recouped the expenditure he had made in the Chillagoe field, but maintained a large block of shares in the Chillagoe Railway and Mines Limited.

The share market looked favourably on Chillagoe. Shares were booming, and 400,000 pounds were raised, principally on the London market. The capital was easy to raise because Reid was an excellent and persuasive company promoter. Stewart, the general manager, had an enviable reputation also, and his report on the Calcifer, Fortunata, Harpers, Mungana, Ortho, Red Cap, Ruddygore, Ti-Tree and Zillmanton mines showed reserves of 508,000 tons of ore containing ten per cent copper. With the formation of the Chillagoe Railway and Mines Limited Company for the purpose of building a railway and smelters at Chillagoe Creek, and a report showing 508,000 tons of readily accessible high-grade ore, there was no stopping the promoters.

The railway from Mareeba to Chillagoe was constructed using the 1892 survey of C A S Andrews. This survey had been initially conducted for Moffat, who wanted to use the land grant system to fulfil his dream of a railway to Chillagoe via his Koorboora mines. However, a deviation through Koorboora was not incorporated in the final track.

Koorboora

The tin deposits at Koorboora, near Irvinebank, were discovered by Anthony Linedale and the Munro brothers in August 1888. In October 1888, John Moffat and Anthony Linedale visited the area while returning from Chillagoe. However, by October 1888 John Moffat had only the Shakespeare lease, and on 12 October 1888 the Munro bothers, Michael Byrnes and John Foy had tied up most of the prospective ground. In 1891, the Irvinebank Mining Company of John Moffat purchased mines from the Munro brothers and sank two shafts on the Shakespeare.

In 1889, there were forty-five men working on the field, a village, a hotel, and the field was producing regular shipments of high-grade cassiterite concentrate. The population dropped to nine during the depression of the early 1890s, despite the discovery of the tungsten mineral wolframite. A rise in the tin price in 1897 encouraged Moffat to shift machinery from his California Creek workings, twenty kilometres south-west of Koorboora. Moffat's crushing and gravity concentrator employed twenty men and treated ores from the Irvinebank Mining Company operations which were carried from the Shakespeare Mine by horse-drawn tram; Moffat also purchased ore for treatment and toll-treated ore from the other operators, to produce a cassiterite concentrate with more than sixty per cent tin.

Koorboora thrived from 1897 until 1927, with maximum production between 1897 and 1911, and the town grew to five hundred inhabitants. The year 1902 saw the discovery of the Neville Mine, which became Australia's richest tungsten mine.

Ore from other tin mines in the district (for example, from Tommy Burns Mine, Sunnymount) was treated. During a period of high tin prices in 1911 there was a four-month strike at Koorboora and later a six-month strike at the Tennyson Mine in 1913–14. These actions were the nail in the coffin for the Koorboora tin field, which enjoyed only marginal profitability despite a few high-grade mines. Production and activity declined and the battery operated spasmodically until final closure in 1927.

The Mareeba to Chillagoe railway

Railway construction began on 6 August 1898. After line clearing from Mareeba to Mungana was completed in October 1900, the workforce of 550 shifted 13,000 cubic metres of material per month and the three-foot-gauge railway line was completed at a cost of 38,902 pounds. Trains were running through to Chillagoe and Mungana in February 1901 and the official opening was on 4 March.

Although the 1887 Mareeba-to-Chillagoe Railway Act stipulated the technical requirements of the Queensland government railways for the construction of the railway, heavy-duty rails were used and concrete culverts rather than timber, while bridges were constructed of steel rather than of wood. In white-ant-infested far north Queensland, such technical wisdom reduced maintenance and enabled heavy trains to negotiate the steep hills and tight corners.

As part of the rather generous Mareeba-to-Chillagoe Railway Act, the company was permitted to charge fifty per cent over government rates, thereby increasing the monopoly on the

Chillagoe field. The daily 6.30 am train from Cairns reached Chillagoe at 4.25 pm and, on Wednesdays and Saturdays, went to the end of the line at Mungana (arrival: 5.15 pm). To the north-west of Chillagoe, the railway was adjacent to the Zillmanton field and was within metres of the Lady Jane and Girofla mines. The terminus at Mungana was, until recently, used as the rail-head for the trucking of cattle. Although the tracks, bridges and railway stations still exist, the railway is now inactive.

Construction of the Chillagoe smelters

The building of the Chillagoe smelters was a long-drawn-out affair. The initial plan by Chapman, Moffat and Reid was to carry ore to the Barron Falls and to smelt it there using hydro-electricity. This source of power was in its infancy but had been successfully used at the Mount Bischoff tin mines (in Tasmania); and Waratah, the town that serviced the mines, had electric lights and electric trams. However, the first Labor government of Queensland, led by Anderson Dawson, was hostile to the Chillagoe promoters. Despite the fact that the Dawson government lasted only seven days, it found a legal technicality which prevented the company erecting a smelter at the Barron Falls. Had a smelter gone ahead as planned there, it might have made the Chillagoe field financially viable.

The Dawson government may have been responding tit-for-tat to the Country–National Party for the generous deal over the railway in 1897 between the latter and the aristocratic promoters of the Chillagoe field who, at that time, were certainly no friends of the Labor Party.

The second option was to build the smelters at Chillagoe, although the developers of the field knew full well that the higher fuel costs involved, and Chillagoe's distance from other fields, would increase the cost of smelting and make the smelters economically vulnerable. The irony to the Dawson government's action was that, in June 1919, the Queensland Labor government of the time acquired the uneconomic railway and smelting concerns at Chillagoe. When the Country–National Party was back in power in 1929, they initiated a Royal Commission and a subsequent civil action against Labor politicians and mining promoters. (See colour plate 33)

Technical experts were appointed to construct the Chillagoe smelters, machinery costing 75,000 pounds was imported and 140,000 pounds were spent on mine development in 1900. There had been a capital expenditure of more than half of the money raised when disaster struck. Metal prices declined and, despite the isolation of the field, there were rumours circulating in the markets that the ore reserves had been grossly over-inflated. Alex Stewart resigned in disgrace and the new general manager (Ernest Albert Weinberg) showed that, without Mungana, the reserves were only 178,000 tons and not 508,000 tons. Weinberg's report was withheld by James Reid while the principals of the company unloaded their stock onto a declining and increasingly suspicious market, and to gain time Weinberg called for a second opinion, using the highly reputed consultant Francis Danvers Powers.

Share scams and mining the market

In September 1901, the Chillagoe smelters were blown in with a great fanfare. Powers' technical report, showing that the estimated reserves were only 96,309 tons – less than a fifth of what had been published only three years before – was submitted in November 1901 and there was a meeting of shareholders in Melbourne that month. For some obscure reason, the shareholders were angry. The directors were censured, but John Moffat was specifically excluded from criticism because he held the same number of shares in November 1901 as he had when the company was incorporated. However, Moffat had sold his vendor's shares in the Chillagoe Proprietary Limited for a substantial profit and had traded heavily in shares in the Chillagoe Railway and Mines Limited Company during 1900. Moffat remained a true believer in Chillagoe and a substantial shareholder, even after the disastrous events of 1901.

Moffat's fellow directors, with their residual minuscule holdings, were pilloried by the shareholders at the Melbourne meeting. These directors had made great profits by insider trading and had sold their stock on a bullish market to unsuspecting investors when the directors were in possession of knowledge that the Chillagoe operations were doomed. But they could not be prosecuted then. Has anything changed? The leaders of scams today still rarely have to face the courts and be responsible for their actions, despite a mountain of corporate, financial, fair trading and consumer legislation.

The company collapsed and the smelters closed at Christmas 1901 after only treating 8529 tons of ore worth 23,792 pounds.

The few remaining assets of the company were reorganised, and the shareholders paid a call of 135,000 pounds to refinance the Chillagoe operations. The New Chillagoe Railway and Mines Limited was the company used for further prospecting, in the hope of identifying more reserves that would allow the profitable reopening of the smelters. More technical staff from Broken Hill were employed and the smelter reopened in October 1902 using ore from the Chillagoe, Mount Garnet and Herberton fields, because there was little ore at Chillagoe. However, the high sphalerite (zinc sulphide) and zinc oxide contents of ore from Mount Garnet created smelting problems, while the flooding of the Zillmanton mines reduced smelter feed, as did the high costs of production at Calcifer and Ruddygore.

Despite the scandals of 1901, James Reid was a director of the New Chillagoe Railway and Mines Limited. With the lack of smelter feed, Reid became desperate and decided to construct a 230-kilometre railway line to the Etheridge mineral field to gain access to more ore. In June 1905, Reid registered the Chillagoe Company Limited for the purpose of building this railway. Reid wanted to expand the smelters using the Huntingdon–Herberlein process against the advice of his general manager, T J Greenway, whom Reid had enticed to Chillagoe from the Broken Hill Junction Company. Greenway resigned in protest and the smelter addition was constructed. With the latest technology and high metal prices, the smelter produced profits of 64,000 pounds and 94,507 pounds in 1907 and 1908 respectively.

But these profits were shortlived. Zillmanton mine was flooded again in the 1911 wet season and on 24 December 1911 much of the Chillagoe smelter was destroyed by fire. Two copper refiners were damaged, the mobile electric crane was ruined and the wooden sleepers of the furnace floor railways were destroyed. The 1912 operating profit of 12,000 pounds was insufficient to pay the interest on the funds raised on the market or to replace the equipment destroyed in the smelter fire. The company was caught between a rock and a hard place. Furthermore, Reid could not use funds raised for the purpose of building the railway line to the Etheridge field, the railway to Mount Mulligan or the Mount Mulligan coal mine, as these funds had already been committed to contractors. Restructuring of the capital of the company into 1,200,000 ten-shilling shares was undertaken in a desperate attempt by Reid to save the enterprise. At the outbreak of World War I, the struggling operations were still uneconomic and were paying interest on a 80,000-pound overdraft.

The third era

In February 1914 the smelters closed once again, despite the prospect of war-induced profitability. The loss of able-bodied human resources to the war guaranteed that the smelters would not reopen in the foreseeable future. James Reid tried to sell the enterprise to the Country–National Party government of Queensland. However, the Premier, Denham, lost power in an election. During the election campaign, the Labor Party had pledged to convert the unsuccessful Chillagoe operations into a state enterprise, but prevarication by Premier Ryan's new

Labor government was such that the idle Chillagoe operations could not capitalise on the high metal prices of World War I. After two Queensland government enquiries and a bill of parliament in November 1918, on 1 January 1919 the Queensland government acquired the Chillagoe smelter for 40,000 pounds, and the railways for 661,000 pounds, as well as the Einasleigh copper mine and associated plant. This purchase led to the infamous Mungana scandal.

The Mungana scandal

The Mungana scandal, a bitter festering sore in Queensland politics between 1926 and 1931, was one of the most widely known in Australian political history. It contributed to the disintegration of the Federal Labor government when Australia was in the grip of the Great Depression, with the resignation on 6 July 1930 by the former Labor Premier of Queensland and the Federal Treasurer, E G Theodore. The scandal ruined the political career not only of 'Red Ted' Theodore (1884–1950) but also of William McCormack (1879–1947; former Queensland Labor premier), N F Macgroarty (Queensland Country–National Party Attorney General) and A D McGill (Chairman of the Country–National Party in Queensland).

The Chillagoe scandal showed that government was unable to run business enterprises such as mining and smelting profitably, and that governments then, as they are now, were incapable of handling conflicts of interest and only too willing to waste public moneys on Royal Commissions and legal challenges as a mechanism of damaging the opposition.

The details of the Mungana scandal have been dealt with by historian K H Kennedy (see Bibliography) and by the historical novelist Frank Hardy, although I outline it below. Hardy's *Power Without Glory*, a highly controversial political exposé initially circulated in 1950 as an illegal book and the subject of a celebrated defamation action, was a thinly veiled *roman à clef*, referring to a Ted Thurgood and the Mulgara Company.

After the Chillagoe company had closed in 1914 the area declined. Then, in 1919, the government of Queensland took over the assets of the Chillagoe and Etheridge Railway, in order to smelt the ore of the local miners. However, a provision of the Legislative Council of Queensland prohibited the government from being a mine owner. 'Red Ted' Theodore was then treasurer in the Queensland Labor government and his lifelong friend McCormack was home secretary. Both had been union organisers in the Chillagoe mining field at Mungana, which had appalling working conditions and a reputation for militant trade unionism. Both had cut their teeth in the school of hard knocks.

With the acquisition of the Chillagoe company's smelters by the Queensland government, the smelter foreman from Mount Elliot (in the Cloncurry mining field), Peter Louis Goddard, was appointed general manager of the Chillagoe smelters.

While the Chillagoe and Etheridge Railway Bill to acquire the assets was before the parliament, local miner Fred Reid had applied to the Department of Mines for the leases covering the Mungana, Lady Jane and Girofla mines. These mines were large producers of ore to the Chillagoe smelters and, with the assistance of Red Ted Theodore, Fred Reid received a Queensland government loan of 3100 pounds to enable the reopening of the mines. At that time, both the State and Federal governments were funding schemes to employ returned soldiers, despite the fact the postwar demand for metals was very low.

The Legislative Council prohibition on government mine ownership was amended in 1920 and the Queensland government acquired the Mungana, Lady Jane and Girofla leases from Fred Reid's company, Mungana Mines Limited, on 25 March 1922 – for a total of 40,000 pounds, comprising 10,000 pounds cash and a royalty of five per cent. The Queensland government spent 41,000 pounds de-watering and rehabilitating Reid's mines, followed by 30,000 pounds in royalties to Reid's Mungana Mines Limited and a further 112,000 pounds in development costs on the leases. Then, in 1926, it was revealed in the press that Home Secretary McCormack held 388 shares in Mungana Mines Ltd, and so he was a beneficiary of the 962,000 pounds invested by the Queensland government in the Chillagoe smelters and associated mines.

The Country–National Party opposition in the Queensland parliament highlighted irregularities in the accounts of the Chillagoe smelters and targeted conflicts of interest. Peter Goddard (General Manager of the Chillagoe smelters), Fred Reid and William McCormack were exposed as beneficiaries of royalties, had interests in the Tarzali sawmill, the Fluorspar Mine and the Argentum Mine, and apparently had used smelter tramway rails in the construction of the Pacific Hotel in Cairns. The Fluorspar Mine was contracted to provide flux to the Chillagoe smelters and the Argentum Mine provided smelter feed. The close commercial relationship between Fred Reid and Peter Goddard led to sweetheart deals and, in order to hose down the bushfire, William McCormack established an enquiry by the Auditor General.

The enquiry provided indicting evidence and, in February 1927, Goddard resigned as the general manager of the Chillagoe smelters. With Goddard's resignation, the smelters closed. Closure of the smelters meant closure of the local mines, as the cost of freighting even high-grade ore to a port, Mount Morgan or Mount Isa was prohibitive.

The Labor Party lost power in Queensland in 1929 and the Country–National Party government of Moore established a Royal Commission to investigate the appointment of Goddard, the corporate interests of Goddard, McCormack and Reid, and the purchase of Mungana Mines Ltd by the Queensland government. A retired New South Wales Supreme Court judge (J L Campbell) commenced the Royal Commission hearing on 30 April 1930 and submitted his report to the Queensland cabinet on 4 July.

Campbell's report concluded that Goddard, McCormack, Reid and Theodore were all guilty of dishonesty and fraud regarding the royalties obtained and the purchase of Mungana Mines Limited by the Queensland government. Theodore resigned as Federal Labor Treasurer two days later.

Under the 1874 Crown Remedies Act, the Queensland government initiated civil proceedings against Goddard, McCormack, Reid and Theodore to recover the monies expended in the purchase of Mungana Mines Ltd. This was a spiteful action, aimed at sending political enemies bankrupt and was clearly not an attempt to seek justice, as despite the Royal Commission conclusions of fraud, the Queensland government did not press criminal proceedings.

The court action under the Crown Remedies Act in July–August 1931 was in front of Chief Justice J W Blair and evolved into a highly charged political affair. The Chairman of the Country–National Party (A D McGill) and George Seaham were barristers for the prosecution and for the defence were A J Mansfield (later Chief Justice and then Governor of Queensland), B H Matthews, N W Macrossan (later appointed a judge) and R F Philip (also later appointed a judge). A jury of four found the defendants not guilty of fraud and conspiracy but the political careers of the two former Queensland Labor Party premiers, Theodore and McCormack, were destroyed. A Not Guilty verdict did not save or exonerate them. A D McGill, one of the prosecuting barristers, so compromised himself that he destroyed his career and damaged the Country–National Party. The Country–National Party Attorney General (N F Macgroarty) fared poorly, as the Not Guilty verdict showed that what appeared to be a political witch hunt had backfired.

While it is true that Goddard and Reid were substantial financial beneficiaries from the arrangement between the Queensland government, Mungana Mines Ltd and the Chillagoe smelters, and McCormack was a beneficiary through his shareholding, albeit small, in Mungana Mines Ltd, it is probable that Theodore did not benefit financially. Theodore, once a union organiser at the Mungana field, was probably more concerned about providing government-sponsored employment for his former union members in postwar times in a remote far north Queensland mining field. I suspect that Theodore was guilty of naive idealism, loyalty to his comrades and ill-conceived pork barrelling.

With all of the brouhaha surrounding Theodore and the attempted discrediting of the Labor Party, it was conveniently forgotten that the passing of the Mareeba-to-Chillagoe Railway Act by the Queensland Country–National Party in November 1897 was an incredibly generous sweetheart deal for the subscribers to the Chillagoe Proprietary Limited.

The smelters were reopened in 1930 and continued operations sporadically until 1943. Subsidies from the Queensland state railways were such that copper ore was transported from Cloncurry to Townsville, from Townsville to Cairns and then from Cairns to the smelters at Chillagoe. The combination of the loss of manpower for World War II, the lack of ore reserves at Chillagoe and the competition from Mount Isa forced closure. In 1943 a fire sale of the buildings, machinery, tools and smelters took place and most of the material had been removed from the site by 1945.

The Mount Isa connection

In the early days of mining in western Queensland, well before the discovery of Mount Isa, John Moffat was investing in mines in the Duchess area of the Cloncurry mining field. A hermit, gold-fossicker and wrongfully-convicted murderer, James Elliott, had discovered cuprite in what was later to be known as Mount Elliott. Elliott lacked capital for mine development, sold his leases to James Morphett, a pastoralist of Fort Constantine, who fell upon hard times during the drought at the turn of the century. The leases were then purchased by John Moffat, who had had the sweet smell of success from his copper mines at

Chillagoe, coal mines at Mount Mulligan and mines in the Northern Territory.

Moffat financed exploration which, by 1907, showed that 45,000 tons of rich copper ore were awaiting extraction. The Mount Elliott field sucked up huge amounts of capital and, despite amalgamation of the workings between 1925 and 1928, the low-grade ore, over-capitalisation and economic downturn resulted in the bankruptcy of the large mining companies. After the demise of the larger companies, small parties of miners gouged out rich copper ore which was freighted by rail 1300 kilometres to the smelters at Chillagoe. This ore was to be the lifeblood of the Chillagoe smelters, which were by then showing symptoms of terminal illness.

In September 1923, geologist Saint-Smith visited the fledgling Mount Isa leases and immediately recognised their potential. A pegging boom started. The Labor government had difficulty with the new field because it was of the view that numerous small miners in a field were preferable to the ownership of a field by one large company. However, ownership by many small operators was uneconomic as infrastructure was duplicated.

Furthermore, it was in the government's interests to freight the Mount Isa ore 1300 kilometres to the ailing state-owned smelters at Chillagoe. The smelters there lacked feed and it was reasoned that the loss on the state-owned railways could be offset by profits on the state-owned smelters. There was some opposition to this concept because it was reported in 1923 that the Nightflower Mine in the Chillagoe field had the same potential as the Mount Isa field, but Saint-Smith's report in

1924 showed that, in contrast to the Mount Isa field, the Night-flower deposit was small and of little potential.

Mount Isa Mines Limited was floated in January 1924. Randolph Bedford, at that time the best-known mining journalist in Australia, floated the Mount Isa Silver Lead Proprietary No Liability in February 1924. Bedford was also a Queensland State Labor politician (the member for Warrego) and enlisted influential associates such as V J Sadler (Director, Silverton Tramway Company at Broken Hill) and Joe Millican (former Charters Towers sharebroker and politician). The largest parcel of shares went to the Melbourne financier John Wren, who is thinly disguised as John West in Frank Hardy's *Power Without Glory*. Bedford gave away shares to media friends at the *Bulletin*, and to other friends including W H Corbould (Director, Mount Isa Mines Limited) and two Cabinet ministers in the Queensland government – Red Ted Theodore and William McCormack. Mount Isa Silver Lead Proprietary No Liability acquired the services of E J J Rodda from Chillagoe, who helped the promoters immeasurably by making statements about the size and grade of the untested orebodies at Mount Isa.

The copper orebodies were found at Mount Isa in 1930. The threat of war and post-depression revival in world trade were such that Mount Isa Mines Limited looked at mining the copper ore at their Black Star and Black Rocks workings and shipping the concentrate to Chillagoe, Port Kembla (New South Wales) or Tacoma (USA) for smelting. These plans were spoiled when the price of copper fell. The decision led to the final demise of the Chillagoe field and its smelters, as the Mount Isa and Cloncurry fields were always the great hope for the survival of the Chillagoe smelters. Very little ore was shipped halfway across Queensland to Chillagoe. Ironically, when the state smelters finally closed at Chillagoe, some ninety skilled smeltermen were relocated to Mount Isa in 1943.

During the height of the mining and smelting operations at Chillagoe, the operating company's influence extended over 25,000 square kilometres, directly affected the lives of 5000 north Queenslanders, and sustained employment in an isolated, economically depressed area.

The smelting process

During the years 1901 to 1943, the Chillagoe smelters were the central location for treatment of ores from the mines in the Chillagoe area such as Calcifer, Red Cap, Ruddygore, Mungana and Zillmanton. Over the life of the smelters, 1.25 million tons of ore were treated for the production of 60,000 tons of copper, 50,000 tons of lead, 181 tons (6.5 million ounces) of silver and 5 tons (175,000 ounces) of gold. Although the ores smelted contained more than ten per cent of these metals, they were also rich in zinc. Market conditions and smelter technology did not allow the building of a separate zinc smelter and the zinc impeded the performance of the smelters. The zinc was lost to the slag. Today, ironically, the zinc mineralisation discovered at Mungana deeps is more valuable than the lead. The inverse was the case in the 1920s.

Roasting

Because the Chillagoe smelters dealt with a great diversity of ore types from numerous mines in the district, the ores required roasting before smelting in order to make the smelter feedstock more uniform. At the time of building, the roasters at Chillagoe were the leading technology in the world and, a century later, Australian mineral processing still leads the world.

In the early days of the Chillagoe field, the ores were high graded during the mining operations and hand-picked before being transported to the small local smelters such as Muldiva, Calcifer and Mungana. With the establishment of the large, centrally located Chillagoe smelters, the high-graded ore was transported to Chillagoe from all the mines in the district.

At Chillagoe, after blending and crushing the fluxes (limestone and fluorite) and ores, the mixture was loaded into sloping hearths. Roasting took place in the Huntingdon–Herberlein roasting plant which was composed of conical kettles and furnaces, using coal as the source of heat. The coal came by rail from the company-owned mines at Mount Mulligan. It was bituminous, produced a large amount of gas and had a high calorific value, but it also had a high ash content. What is not commonly known is that, in the 1920s, Mount Mulligan was the site of Australia's largest mine accident. The coal that was so valued for the smelters because of its high gas content came from mines where the same gas could build up dangerously underground; the gas exploded at Mount Mulligan, killing seventy-four miners.

During roasting, air was passed through the roaster to oxidise the sulphide ore minerals, the main one being pyrite. The conversion of sulphide minerals to sulphur dioxide released heat which assisted the roasting process, while sulphur dioxide from the sulphide ores escaped up a chimney. This emission of sulphur dioxide into the atmosphere created a fallout of sulphuric acid around the smelter. The bleaching of limestones within the town of Chillagoe is a result of solution of the limestone by the intense acid rainfall derived from the sulphuric acid. The evidence can still be seen in Chillagoe, more than fifty years after the smelting operations ceased.

Smelting

The roasted ore was carried by train to the smelter. After sampling, to measure its sulphur and metal content, it was stored in hoppers adjacent to the coke. (Because coal from the company's coal mines at Mount Mulligan contained such a high gas content, it was used to make coke. In smelting, the physical strength, the porosity and enhanced chemical features of coke over coal make it an ideal additive for smelting.) Feeding both coke and roasted ore from the hoppers into the smelters allowed blending of the coke, depending upon the metal and sulphur content of the roasted ore.

Fluxes were added to the ore during smelting, as these lowered the melting temperature and so made smelting easier. Because the ore was crushed with the flux to a coarse-grain size and because the coke was porous, hot gas was able to flow up. The solid roasted ore, flux and coke gravitated to the base of the smelter. The coke acted as both a source of heat and to convert roasted ore minerals to molten metals by chemical reduction. The heavy, molten copper or lead was tapped from the bottom of the furnace and water-cooled. The slag was tapped from higher up in the furnace. Exhaust gases were sulphur dioxide, carbon monoxide, arsenic oxides and fluorides.

Refining

The impure copper contained lead and minor amounts of silver, cobalt and gold, whereas the impure lead contained copper and minor amounts of silver, bismuth, antimony and arsenic. The impure copper and lead were refined in separate furnaces. By using additives and accurately controlling the temperature of the molten metals in the furnaces, producers could separate the copper from the precious metals. In the lead furnaces, the lead was separated from the copper, bismuth, antimony and arsenic which concentrated in the scum (dross) on the top of the molten lead. The use of additives enabled molten silver to be separated from the molten lead. Copper, lead, silver and gold were poured into separate moulds and stored in the smelter strongroom adjacent to the main offices before rail transportation to the markets. Waste gases rich in arsenic, antimony and sulphur went up the main chimney. Because the chimney top was seventy-three metres above the smelter floor, the chimney drew well and waste gases were widely dispersed from the top of the southern hill.

The large smelting operation was supported by workshops for blacksmiths, carpenters and fitters. A powerhouse, which had its own chimney for waste gases, burned coal for the production of steam in boilers. Behind the powerhouse were water tanks for cooling water and for steam production. The steam drove turbines for the generation of electricity, which was used to power electric cranes to carry pots of molten metal from one part of the smelter to another, and for energy for metal refining, for machinery and for lighting.

Slag

The molten slag was tapped into bell-shaped cones and transported by hand-pushed and horse-drawn railway wagons from the smelters to the slag dump on narrow-gauge railways. The bells were overturned and the molten slag poured out on the slag heap. Streams of black slag flowed over the edge of the heap, cementing pieces of slag together and developing a ropy texture. In many places on the slag dump small streams and creeks of slag can be seen today.

The surface of the slag cooled quickly to a lustrous black glass which often had an iridescent coating. The larger masses of slag cooled more slowly. Crystals started to grow in the cooling, molten slag, which finally solidified as glass. The same features are seen in modern and ancient lavas. (See colour plate 34)

The black slags from the Chillagoe smelters are composed of a number of synthetic minerals and glass. Synthetic olivine, spinel, feldspar, iron oxide and bornite have been observed in the slag.

Although the Chillagoe smelters at the time of operation were 'state of the art', not all of the metal was extracted during processing. Molten silicates and molten sulphides do not mix with each other; they are like oil and water. The heavy molten sulphide sinks in the molten silicates and is converted to metal by coke reduction. The molten metal was tapped from the bottom of the furnace. However, if the smelting process was undertaken too quickly or the smelter was being blown in, then not all the molten sulphide sank and some was preserved as small spheres in the slag. These spheres of sulphide are now oxidised to malachite.

Although the slags from Chillagoe contain less than 0.1 per cent copper and 0.5 per cent zinc, they represent a gold resource as the 250,000 tons of slag there still contain more than four grams per ton of gold.

Mineralogy of slag

The most common synthetic mineral in the slag is an olivine mineral. It occurs as long needle-like crystal intergrowths in the slag, indicative of very rapid cooling. The synthetic olivine is an iron–calcium silicate with minor amounts of magnesium and zinc present. The iron derives from the smelting of the copper–iron sulphides, the calcium from the addition of fluorite and limestone as fluxes to lower melting point, and the silica from the silica in the smelted ores. The magnesium in the synthetic olivine derives from the magnesium minerals diopside and hedenbergite in the smelted ore. The zinc sulphide mineral sphalerite was a common minor mineral in the ores smelted at Chillagoe. In nature, zinc forms sulphide, silicate and oxide minerals. During smelting, the sulphur was driven up the smelter stack and the small amounts of zinc went into the synthetic olivine and synthetic spinel found in the slag.

Synthetic spinel from the slag is an iron aluminium oxide with minor amounts of magnesium, zinc, titanium and chromium. The iron, magnesium, titanium and possibly chromium derive from silicate minerals such as garnet, hedenbergite, diopside and chlorite, whereas the aluminium derives from clays and feldspars in the ore. Synthetic plagioclase feldspar (calcium aluminium silicate) in the slag contains minor sodium and potassium. Rare crystals of iron oxide contain minor aluminium, magnesium, calcium and manganese.

Between the elongate crystals of the silicate minerals is black glass, similar in composition to a natural iron-rich basalt.

The silicate glass from the Chillagoe slag contains 39 to 44 per cent silica, with major quantities of iron, calcium and aluminium and significant quantities of sodium and potassium. There are trace amounts of zinc, magnesium, manganese, titanium, fluorine, chlorine, phosphorus and sulphur. The major components of the glass derive from the molten silicate minerals in the ore, as do the magnesium, manganese and titanium. The zinc and sulphur derive from the sulphide ores and the fluorine from the fluorite (calcium fluoride) flux. Fossil remains in the limestone flux contributed the phosphorus and chlorine.

The fourth era

Since 1943, despite the spectacular corporate failures, the share market scams, the lack of reserves and the unprofitability of the smelters which resulted in the closure of the smelters, the Chillagoe field has attracted the attention of mineral exploration groups. Ironically, after a two-million-dollar expenditure by Amoco Minerals (later Cyprus Minerals) on John Moffat's original leases at Lady Jane, Magazine Face, Girofla and Griffiths Hill, a gold resource of 17.5 million tons of ore with a grade of 2.6 grams per ton was identified to a depth of 170 metres. These mines had previously produced 340,000 tons of ore, from which 32,000 tons of lead, 8000 tons of copper and 3.75 million ounces of silver were extracted during smelting. However, the gold potential had not previously been recognised and there had been only limited surface gouging for secondary copper minerals at Red Dome. With a free-market gold price producing strong metal prices, and the advent of carbon-in-pulp technology which efficiently extracted gold from low-grade ores, the potential profit looked interesting, and as a result Mungana Mines Limited was formed in 1983 and sold to Elders IXL in 1985 for six million dollars.

Mine construction began in February 1986 and Australia's first heap leach mine poured its first gold on 20 June 1986. Over nine years of operation by Elders IXL, the mine produced an average of 160 kilograms of gold per month as a result of leaching heaps of two-grams-per-ton ore with dilute sodium cyanide. Sodium cyanide reacts with gold to produce gold cyanide, which in turn reacts with granular activated carbon. The carbon strips the gold from the gold cyanide, which reacts back to sodium cyanide and is recycled in the plant. The gold-bearing activated carbon granules are collected, gold is chemically stripped from the activated carbon and the carbon heated to reactivate before use again. The gold is smelted to dore, a gold–silver alloy, which is sent to a refinery.

After most of the oxidised ore amenable to heap leaching had been exploited, a new process was required to treat the deeper, mineralogically complex sulphide ore. Thus, in 1989, a new grinding, flotation and carbon-in-pulp plant was commissioned.

In March 1991, Niugini Mining Ltd purchased the Red Dome Mine from Elders IXL. The mine is currently operating at an annual production rate of approximately 100,000 ounces of gold, 360,000 ounces of silver and 4600 tons of copper. The Red Dome open pit is in its third stage and has been deepened a further 90 metres to approximately 300 metres beneath the original land surface. The third stage of development of the

Red Dome Mine involved a capital injection of $42 million to be recouped by 1997. Since 1986, some 100 million tons of rock have been removed from Red Dome, for the treatment of 10 million tons of ore, yielding 1 million ounces of gold.

The Red Dome open pit is the steepest and deepest open-pit mine in Australia. It is more than 300 metres deep and its high walls have slopes up to seventy degrees. It is a spectacular engineering feat. To keep such a massive pit workable, when it must sustain an annual monsoonal battering and the mining of very metallurgically-complex ore in a complicated geological terrain, is a credit to the engineering, metallurgical and geological professionalism at Red Dome. (See colour plate 35)

The complexity of the ore is such that Niugini Mining Ltd have had to devise new metallurgical techniques for the treatment of the 3300 tons per day. The mine employs more than 200 staff and contractors and is a significant economic contributor to the economy of far north Queensland. The Red Dome Mine has won the Premier's Award for Environmental Excellence, provides funds for community projects and road development, and funds research on tailings dam studies, ecological and hydrological research, and archaeological and historical scholarship.

The fifth era

Over the past five decades, cattle and tourism have been the lifeblood of Chillagoe. However, with the latest ore-treatment technology and excellent sustained exploration, new mineral resources have been identified and Chillagoe's colourful mining heritage will continue. Through the use of modern technology, creative thinking and risk-taking, new gold and base metal resources have been identified at Mungana, Mungana deeps, Girofla and Lady Jane – John Moffat's original leases. Other areas, such as the old mines at Shannon, Zillmanton and Harpers, are undergoing reinvestigation for new types of deposits at depth. Virgin occurrences of gold, such as at Mungana and Arachnid, are also making the Chillagoe area an exciting new gold province.

The first three eras of prospecting and mining at Chillagoe concentrated on copper and lead. The fourth era used modern technology and was able to exploit both copper and gold. Although the mineral exploration underpinning the new, fifth, era was directed at identifying gold or gold–copper deposits in the Chillagoe district, the exploration results have been far more encouraging. Gold and gold–copper deposits were discovered at Mungana in very complex rocks, as were high-grade massive sulphides of zinc–lead–copper–silver. The base metal sulphides are overprinted by a geological event that deposited gold. These metal-bearing rocks were remobilised and again overprinted by base metals (with carbonate minerals) before the whole area was fragmented by steam explosions.

One of these discoveries, the Mungana gold and base metal deposit, is only one kilometre north of Mungana, yet was discovered in the 1990s in an intensely prospected mineral field. Although the gold deposit is in outcrop, the gold content was far too low to be of interest to miners in the first three eras. There is no outcrop of the base metal deposit and it was only found by persistence and clever science. (See colour plage 36)

Late last century, John Moffat used experienced and talented prospecting teams to open up the Chillagoe field and late this century Niugini Mining Ltd also used an experienced and talented exploration group to find more mineral resources. Both John Moffat and Niugini Mining Ltd have been successful. These new resources are within trucking or underground mining distance of the Red Dome metallurgical plant and the Chillagoe field is now on the point of entering its fifth era of mining, following the exhaustion of the Red Dome open pit. Mining there has now ceased, but the stockpiled ore will enable the mill to operate until late 1997.

After that plans are being made to mine the unexploited underground reserves at Red Dome, while the Griffiths Hill deposit is also poised to produce copper and gold. New types of gold deposits have been identified in virgin prospects and old flooded mines which were once regarded as prospective for copper. At depth the Mungana field has shallow copper–gold deposits, a number of types of gold deposits, and deep copper–zinc deposits.

Although production costs soar for underground mining at great depth as compared to open pits, and the takeover by Niugini Mining Ltd of Battle Mountain Gold has left some uncertainty about future directions, we can hope that the Chillagoe field will not once again fall silent. All the resources that are present in the ground should mean the Chillagoe mineral field has an exciting future. I, for one, look forward to its fifth era.

GLOSSARY OF
CHILLAGOE MINERALS

Acanthite Ag_2S, monoclinic. Rare microscopic grains have been observed from Chillagoe. See argentite.

Actinolite $Ca_2(Mg,Fe)_5Si_8O_{22}(OH)_2$, monoclinic. Green fibrous amphibole mineral typical of metamorphosed impure limestone and common from Chillagoe.

Adularia $KAlSi_3O_8$, triclinic. A low-temperature variety of microcline which typically forms from boiling fluid. Difficult to identify in hand specimen and normally seen only by staining the rock with sodium cobalitnitrate.

Aikinite $PbCuBiS_3$, orthorhombic. Rare and seen only under the microscope.

Altaite $PbTe$, cubic. One of the few tellurium minerals in nature. Rare and seen only under the microscope.

Alunite $KAl_3(SO_4)_2(OH)_6$, trigonal. Reportedly rare from Chillagoe but the difficulty in identification is such that it is probably common. Chillagoe hand specimens are flinty-to-waxy pinkish-to-orange masses. Typically forms in acid oxidised conditions.

Amphibole A family of water-bearing ferromagnesian silicates. See actinolite and tremolite.

Andradite $Ca_3Fe_2(SiO_4)_3$, cubic. A member of the garnet family, typically brown–black. Forms euhedral crystals and forms in oxidised metamorphic rocks. Very common from Chillagoe. Some good collectors' specimens from the Red Dome pit where the garnet is hosted by calcite.

Anglesite $PbSO_4$, orthorhombic. Bladed white dense crystals, commonly associated with oxides of iron and copper carbonates. Rare from Chillagoe.

Ankerite $Ca(Fe,Mg,Mn)(CO_3)_2$, trigonal. Rare orange–brown carbonate with typical rhombic cleavage. Quickly oxidises at surface and along rhombic cleavages to iron oxides.

Argentite Ag_2S, cubic. Although argentite is recorded in the literature and in Chillagoe collections, this mineral is stable only above 177 degrees Celsius. Argentite is really acanthite.

Arsenopyrite $FeAsS$, monoclinic. Rare. When struck, smells of garlic. Looks orthorhombic, silvery. Occurs in quartz veins as isolated crystals and associated with gold and pyrite.

Azurite $Cu_3(CO_3)_2(OH)_2$, monoclinic. Common. Deep azure–blue bladed crystals commonly partially pseudomorphed by malachite or pitted crystals. Chillagoe is world famous for its azurite, much of which was recently extracted from the upper levels of the Red Dome open pit.

Baryte (barite) $BaSO_4$, orthorhombic. Dense white-bladed or stellate crystals. Rare.

Bertherine $(Fe,Al)_3(Si,Al)_2O_5(OH)_4$. A rare layered silicate mineral belonging to the serpentine family, visible only under the microscope.

Biotite $K(Mg,Fe)_3(Al,Fe)Si_3O_{10}(OH,F)_2$, monoclinic. Very common brown-to-black platey mica.

Bismuth Bi, trigonal. Rare. Metallic, tarnishes rapidly and visible only under the microscope.

Bismuthinite Bi_2S_3, orthorhombic. Rare. Fibrous, visible only under the microscope.

Bornite Cu_5FeS_4, cubic. Very common at Chillagoe. When fresh, massive and chestnut-brown; however, very rapidly tarnishes to 'peacock ore' comprising a play of coloured oxidised phases on the surface of the bornite. Occurs within calc-silicate rocks, associated with chalcopyrite.

Brochantite $Cu_4(SO_4)(OH)_6$, monoclinic. Rare. Fibrous emerald green.

Calcite $CaCO_3$, trigonal. Common. White, rhomboidal cleavage blocks as crystals lining cavities or massive. Occurs as a primary mineral of the calc-silicate rocks, in veins and fractures, and as coatings on other minerals such as malachite.

Cassiterite SnO_2, tetragonal. Rare. Visible only under the microscope.

Cerussite $PbCO_3$, orthorhombic. Rare. Small-bladed, twinned, stellate or swallow tail crystals. Adamantine and commonly coated by anglesite.

Chalcocite Cu_2S, monoclinic. No record of crystals from Chillagoe. Massive silvery blue to sooty. One of the more common ore minerals from Chillagoe.

Chalcopyrite Cu_5FeS_4, tetragonal. Very common. Massive, brassy yellow, commonly tarnished to a 'peacock ore' play of colours. Occurs in calc-silicate rocks associated with bornite.

Chalcotrichtite Not a valid mineral species. See cuprite.

Chillagite Not a valid mineral species. See (tungstian) wulfenite.

Chlorite a complex group of monoclinic and triclinic water-bearing silicates of iron, magnesium and aluminium. Common. Dark green, platey to massive.

Chrysocolla $(Cu,Al)_2H_2Si_2O_5(OH)_4.nH_2O$, monoclinic. Common. Variable green to blue. When containing manganese, is a lustrous black. Occurs in cracks, as coatings and massive. Never crystalline.

Cobaltite CoAsS, orthorhombic. Rare silvery white. Visible only under the microscope.

Copper (native) Cu, cubic. Common from Chillagoe, copper-red, sectile, commonly coated with black oxides and associated with cuprite. Can be filiform, dendritic, massive or crystalline.

Cuprite Cu_2O, cubic. Common. Crystals are port wine red, lustrous and transparent, whereas massive cuprite is red.

Cuspidine $Ca_4Si_2O_7(F,OH)_2$, monoclinic.

Diamond C, cubic. The very rare and hardest known mineral in nature.

Dickite $Al_2Si_2O_5(OH)_4$, monoclinic. Same chemistry as kaolinite but different structure. A clay mineral that generally forms in hot acid conditions.

Diopside $CaMgSi_2O_6$, monoclinic. A common deep green coloured calc-silicate pyroxene mineral. Normally massive and rarely crystalline from Chillagoe. Occurs in calc-silicate rocks, veins and altered porphyry dykes.

Djurleite $Cu_{31}S_{16}$, monoclinic. Very similar to chalcocite. Detected under the microscope only by means of X-rays.

Emplectite $CuBiS_2$, orthorhombic. Rare. Visible under the microscope.

Epidote $Ca_2(Fe,Al)_3(SiO_4)_3(OH)$, monoclinic. Common bright-green calc-silicate mineral, associated with garnet, diopside, hedenbergite and plagioclase. In veins, masses and as pseudomorphs.

Erthyrite $Co_3(AsO_4)_2.8H_2O$, monoclinic. 'Cobalt bloom', pink-to-red stainings, coatings and veins in weathered rock, rare fibrous stellate crystal masses.

Feldspar two families of minerals comprising the plagioclases $(CaAl_2Si_2O_8-NaAlSi_3O_8)$ and alkali feldspars (microcline, orthoclase, sanidine, adularia $(K,Na)AlSi_3O_8$).

Ferrobustamite $Ca(Fe,Ca,Mn)Si_2O_6$, triclinic. Rare. Red, fibrous to massive.

Fluorite CaF_2, cubic. A common mineral from the Chillagoe district. Massive, cubic and octahedral cleaved blocks. Colourless, blue, green and orange.

Galena PbS, cubic. Massive to crystalline. Occurs in veins, masses and cavities. Commonly cubes, rare octahedra.

Glaucodot $(Co,Fe)AsS$, orthorhombic. Very similar to arsenopyrite. Rare. Identified under the microscope.

Gold (native) Au, cubic. Although the Red Dome Mine was a gold producer, gold is very rare. Alloyed with silver. Generally visible only under the microscope.

Grossular $Ca_3Al_2(SiO_4)_3$, cubic. Common lime-green-to-brown garnet from the calc-silicate rocks at Chillagoe. Euhedral crystals common.

Haematite (Hematite) Fe_2O_3, trigonal. Common iron oxide, rarely as specular lustrous black crystals, more commonly as red, orange and brown masses impregnating other minerals and rocks.

Hedenbergite $CaFeSi_2O_6$, monoclinic. Common dark-green-to-black massive calc-silicate mineral, associated with garnet. Occurs in calc-silicate rocks and altered porphyry dykes.

Hessite Ag_2Te, monoclinic. Very rare. Visible only under the microscope.

Illite a family of mica-like clay minerals with the general formula of $(K,H_3O)(Al,Mg,Fe)_2(Si,Al)_4O_{10}.Nh_2O$. Massive, disseminated and does not occur as crystals. Common but can be identified only by X-ray diffraction.

Ilmenite $FeTiO_3$, trigonal. Rare, occurs as microscopic-sized crystals in many of the granitic rocks and sediments derived therefrom.

Jasper Not a mineral. Massive cryptocrystalline quartz-coloured black, red, orange and yellow by iron oxides.

Joseite Bi_4TeS_4, trigonal. Very rare. Visible only under the microscope.

Kaolinite $Al_2Si_2O_5(OH)_4$, trigonal. Very common as white-to-iron-stained masses in altered and weathered rocks. No crystals found from Chillagoe.

Libethinite $Cu_2(PO_4)(OH)$, orthorhombic. A rare mineral but common from Chillagoe as green minerals from the area all tend to be called malachite. Darker green than malachite, does not pseudomorph azurite and occurs as crystals, stellate masses and tufts with iron oxides, calcite and clays.

Limonite an extremely common mixture of hydrous and anhydrous iron oxides. Not a mineral but commonly contains a high proportion of goethite. Occurs massive, pseudomorphous, cavernous and botryoidal aggregates in all weathered rocks from Chillagoe.

Malachite $Cu_2(CO_3)(OH)_2$, monoclinic. Very common from Chillagoe as bright-green radiating crystal masses, massive, encrustations, veins and pseudomorphs after azurite, cuprite and native copper.

Magnetite Fe_3O_4, cubic. Magnetic iron oxide occurs as small grains in granites, isolated crystals in calc-silicate masses and massive magnetite in marble.

Marcasite FeS_2, orthorhombic. Rare pale-yellowish crystals associated with other massive sulphides. Commonly visible only under the microscope.

Meneghinite $Pb_{13}CuSb_7S_{24}$, orthorhombic. Visible only under the microscope.

Mica A family of water-bearing potassium aluminium silicates.

Molybdenite MoS_2, hexagonal. Rare silver plates in quartz, most commonly seen under the microscope.

Montmorillonite $(Na,Ca)_{0.3}(Al,Mg)_2Si_4O_{10}(OH)_2.nH_2O$, monoclinic. Occurs as masses and in veins, greasy, greenish white but commonly stained by iron oxides. Identified by X-rays or swelling/shrinking characteristics.

Muscovite $KAl_2(Si_3Al)O_{10}(OH,F)_2$, monoclinic. Plates, veins and aggregates of silvery grains associated with granite.

Nontronite $Na_{0.3}Fe_2(Si,Al)_4O_{10}(OH)_2.nH_2O$, monoclinic. Bright-green, greasy, swelling/shrinking clay found in fault zones and veins in the Red Dome open pit.

Olivine $MgSiO_4/FeSiO_4$ family of orthorhombic silicates. Fayalite, $FeSiO_4$, very common in Chillagoe smelter slag.

Orthoclase $KAlSi_3O_8$, monoclinic. Pink-to-white tabular crystals and aggregates in granites and volcanic rocks in the Chillagoe area. Commonly slightly altered by haematite inclusions to brick-red feldspars or partially replaced by clays and micas.

Plagioclase $CaAl_2Si_2O_8$, monoclinic. White crystalline masses in granites and volcanic rocks in the Chillagoe district. Normally altered to a mixture of epidote group minerals, micas and clays.

Plumbogummite $PbAl_3(PO_4)_2(OH)_5.H_2O$, trigonal. Yellowish earthy masses and encrustations in limonite.

Pseudomalachite $Cu_5(PO_4)_2(OH)_4$, monoclinic. Dark green. As the name suggests, often confused with malachite. Does not pseudo-morph azurite, cuprite or native copper and occurs associated with cavernous iron oxides and calcite.

Pyrite FeS_2, cubic. Common mineral from the Chillagoe district as cubes, octahedra and massive pyrite associated with sphalerite and galena. Rare from Red Dome. Only a few excellent display specimens are known from Chillagoe.

Pyrrhotite FeS, monoclinic. Pyrrhotite is rare, associated with massive pyrite, sphalerite and galena, massive, commonly seen under the microscope.

Quartz SiO_2, trigonal. Ubiquitous. Massive, saccharoidal, crystalline, veins, coatings and as cavity linings. Commonly milky white but can be pink, red, yellow, orange and brown. Only a few excellent display specimens are known from Chillagoe.

Rhodochrosite $MnCO_3$, trigonal. Rare. Occurs as late-stage veins and infillings associated with pyrite, galena and sphalerite. Weathering imparts a brown-to-black coating.

Sapphire Al_2O_3, hexagonal. Not recorded from Chillagoe. Present in alluvium draining from basalts in the Great Dividing Range. Blue, green and colourless hexagonal crystals, barrel-shaped to tapering.

Scheelite $CaWO_4$, tetragonal. Minor, massive, white, dispersed mineral in calc-silicate rocks and quartz veins. Detected only under the microscope, in heavy mineral concentrates or under UV light.

Sericite Fine-grained 'white' mica, usually muscovite but can also more rarely be illite or paragonite.

Siderite $FeCO_3$, trigonal. Rare. Occurs as cleaved masses late stage veins and infillings associated with pyrite, galena and sphalerite. Weathering to black rhomboidal limonite masses.

Silver (native) Ag, cubic. Rare. Most commonly alloyed with gold in the primary bornite-chalcopyrite ore from Red Dome. Rare supergene wire silver occurs on limonite in cracks and cavities.

Sphalerite (Zn,Fe)S, cubic. Black iron-bearing, massive, cleaved, aggregates. Rare from Red Dome open pit, common from Mungana where it is associated with pyrite and galena.

Stannite Cu_2FeSnS_4, tetragonal. Rare. Visible only under the microscope.

Stibnite Sb_2S_3, orthorhombic. Rare fibrous metallic crystals and crystal aggregates have been found lining cavities in the Red Dome open pit.

Stolzite $PbWO_4$, tetragonal. The series wulfenite ($PbMoO_4$)–stolzite is a tetragonal solid solution series within which the discredited mineral 'chillagite' is a mid point. Stolzite, wulfenite and 'chillagite' are yellowish-orange platey-to-stubby crystals found only in highly oxidised cavernous limonitic material.

Tellurium Te, trigonal. A very rare mineral, seen only under the microscope.

Tellurobismutite Bi_2Te_3, trigonal. A very rare mineral, seen only under the microscope.

Tennantite $(Cu,Fe)_{12}As_4S_{13}$, cubic. Rare late-stage mineral associated with galena and sphalerite.

Tenorite CuO, monoclinic. Black, massive coatings to cuprite and native copper. Very common from the Red Dome open pit.

Tetradymite Bi_2Te_2S, trigonal. A very rare mineral seen only under the microscope.

Tetrahedrite $(Cu,Fe)_{12}Sb_4S_{13}$, cubic. Rare late-stage mineral associated with galena and sphalerite.

Vesuvianite $Ca_{10}Mg_2Al_4(SiO_4)_5(Si_2O_7)_2(OH)_4$, tetragonal. Rare brown fibrous mineral in the calc-silicate rocks from the Red Dome open pit.

Wollastonite $CaSiO_3$, monoclinic. Rare white-bladed mineral from the calc-silicate rocks of the Red Dome open pit.

Wulfenite $PbMoO_4$, tetragonal. The series wulfenite-stolzite $(PbWO_4)$ is a tetragonal solid-solution series within which the discredited mineral 'chillagite' is a mid point. Stolzite, wulfenite and 'chillagite' are yellowish-orange platey-to-stubby crystals found only in highly oxidised cavernous limonitic material.

Zircon $ZrSiO_4$, tetragonal. Common accessory mineral in the granites of the Chillagoe area.

BIBLIOGRAPHY

Blainey, G., 1960. *Mines in the Spinifex*. Angus and Robertson, Sydney

Hardy, Frank. J., 1950. *Power Without Glory*. Reprinted Lloyd O'Neil (1972)

Kennedy, K. H., 1978. *The Mungana Affair—State Mining and Political Corruption in the 1920s*. University of Queensland Press

Kerr, Ruth S., 1986. *Chillagoe—Copper, Cattle and Caves*. Albion Press

Woodbury, M. J., 1994. 'Red Dome & Mungana porphyry Cu-Au and base metal skarns of north east Queensland.' BSc (Hons) thesis, Australian National University, Canberra